THE CURIOUS TRAVELER

See the world. Change your life.

David Livermore

Cultural Intelligence Center, LLC
Grand Rapids, Michigan

©2019 David Livermore

Published by Cultural Intelligence Center, LLC
678 Front Avenue NW, Ste. 340
Grand Rapids, Michigan 49504

Printed in the United States of America. All rights reserved.

CQ is a trademark of the Cultural Intelligence Center, LLC.

Library of Congress, Cataloging-in-Publication Data
Livermore, David A., 1967-
The curious traveler: See the world. Change your life./David Livermore
p. cm.
ISBN (paperback): 978-1-7340433-0-3
IBSN (eBook): 978-1-7340433-1-0
1. Cultural intelligence. 2. Travel. 3. Cross-cultural orientation. 4. Intercultural communication. 5. National characteristics. I. Title
Library of Congress Control Number: 2019914947

ABOUT THE CULTURAL INTELLIGENCE CENTER
We help individuals and organizations build bridges and remove barriers for working and relating across cultures.

Cover Design: Grace Livermore
Inside Design: Amie McCracken

To my mother

Your faithful, optimistic, curious spirit lives on.

All my love ...

CONTENTS

Prologue

I never left North America until I was 19. My family was a road trip family. We drove just about everywhere—Florida, New England, the West Coast. Going international meant crossing the border to Canada where the rest of our family lived. Traveling overseas never entered my mind until I studied abroad in college. Then I was hooked. I was mesmerized by the smells and sounds, the colorful money, and the alarming sight of police armed with machine guns at traffic lights. Most of all, I was captivated by the people I encountered who grew up a world apart from me.

Fast-forward a few decades, and my kids have been on every continent except Antarctica—all before they graduated from high school. They've tagged along on work trips to China, Japan, and South Africa. We've spent spring breaks in Guatemala and Argentina and Christmases in Myanmar and India. But it's not about airplanes and bragging rights. It's the experiences we've had to meet and connect with so many fascinating people along the way.

Heading overseas for a couple weeks is no longer an anomaly. Whether it's spring break in Cuba, studying abroad in Ghana, or landing a job that allows for travel, the desire to see and experience the world firsthand is at an all-time high. Around 1.3 billion international travelers spend $10 trillion annually on travel. At his Harvard commencement address, Facebook founder Mark Zuckerberg said, "Millennials are the first generation to truly understand themselves as global citizens. They want to make a difference in the world, they're concerned about human rights, and they want to travel."[1]

I rarely meet someone who doesn't love to travel. But many hold back because they're fearful of the unknown or the expense. Travel surprises you, challenges you, scares you, and confronts you. It inspires us to ask bigger, deeper, more probing questions about our world and ourselves. It can change you forever.

I want to give you a different way to think about travel. The difference is rooted in your ability to harness your curiosity with cultural intelligence. I'm not going to bore you with lists of what you should and shouldn't do abroad. You're unlikely to remember those, and many of those lists stem from outdated stereotypes anyway.

The first couple of chapters look at some of the research behind this culturally intelligent, curious mindset I want you to take with you overseas. Then we'll explore some of the dilemmas inevitably faced by international travelers like you and me. These are things like *Why do people always cut in line here? Should I eat the eye?* and *Why would someone give me the wrong directions instead of just telling me they don't know?* The point isn't really to answer the questions as much as to learn how to think through these kinds of dilemmas to see things about yourself and others you may otherwise miss. And finally, I'll share some practical guidelines for how to use the innate power of curiosity to make your travels richer.

St. Augustine of Hippo is famously quoted as saying, "The world is a book and those who do not travel read only one page." As more of us travel for work, study, and recreation, curiosity and travel offer an unmatched resource to teach us about ourselves and others. A curious approach to travel can bridge the way you work and relate with people from the other side of the world. It can remove the barriers between next-door neighbors and coworkers with different political views. And it has the power to make you smarter and help you solve problems big and small.

What a great time to be alive. We can get most anywhere in the world within one to two days. Wheels up. Let's do this!

Part I
Pack Your Curiosity and Cultural Intelligence (CQ)

Curiosity can instantly connect you with anyone. It's what sets us apart from robots, and it's a key factor behind curing cancer, stopping terrorism, and resolving interpersonal conflicts. Meanwhile, international travel is the ideal laboratory for developing and applying your curiosity.

I want to equip you to leverage the power of curiosity and travel to make you happier, to connect with others, and to solve problems big and small as you travel. Part I lays the foundation for how to leverage the power of curiosity to make the most of travel both in the moment and long after you're back home. I'm going to give you some science-based insights for how to spark curiosity in yourself and others, and you'll learn how to direct your curiosity with cultural intelligence. You already know what curiosity is. And cultural intelligence is the capability to relate and work effectively in different cultural contexts. Let's see what we can learn from the research behind these ideas.

1

THE POWER OF CURIOSITY

Over the last decade, my colleagues and I have surveyed over 150,000 individuals from more than 100 countries. The question we've been exploring is this: *What's the difference between those who can relate and work effectively with people from different cultures versus those that stumble and fail?* In other words, who are the culturally intelligent? Our findings indicate there is only one consistent characteristic among every culturally intelligent individual. It's not where you grew up, how many languages you speak, whether you're part of an underrepresented group, or how far you've traveled. It's your curiosity. A curious traveler is one who encounters a different perspective, leans in, pauses, and thinks, *Hmm ... I wonder why that is.*

Curiosity, travel, and cultural intelligence are the perfect combination to see things about yourself and others you may otherwise miss. When you encounter the people and places of the world up close, you open yourself up to a whole new world. It's a world that can't be learned in a classroom or by watching the latest movie. And I'm going to tell you how to get the most from your travels near and far.

I'm insatiably curious. I often look at the person sitting across from me on the airplane and wonder what their life consists of. Or I talk with a group of intelligence analysts and find myself completely fascinated by the work they do and the things they know and will never be able to tell me. I'm intrigued by what is truly going on in the mind of my aging mother who rarely discloses her feelings or emotions to me. When I get hooked on a new TV show, I start googling the lead actors to find out who they are in real life.

My family shares my sense of curiosity. We've had the enormous privilege of traveling and living abroad. Ever since our kids were very young, we've had a rule among us as we encounter different cultures. Unfamiliar behaviors or customs are not "weird" or "wrong" but *different*. This has never been about instilling politically correctness. It's about creating a mindset that looks for what's novel and interesting about the unfamiliar rather than rushing to judgment or feeling defensive.

The first time we were served spicy noodles for breakfast in Southeast Asia, my wife and I told our kids to think of the experience as *different* from the cereal we typically eat for breakfast, not *weird* or *wrong*. And we used it as an opportunity to think about why cereal seems normal to us and why noodles seem normal for so many others. But it was my kids who enforced our family rule when we were driving through a rural Michigan town one day that was celebrating its annual asparagus festival. As a native New Yorker, I scoffed at the whole idea of an asparagus festival as just downright "weird," and my kids immediately responded, "*Weird*, Dad?"

Wherever you are right now, look at something around you and ask, *Hmm … I wonder why that is?* It's a question used by anthropologists when they enter a new culture, but it's useful in familiar environments as well.[1] Why was the building you're in right now originally built? Who decided to build it? How did the couple living around the corner end up together? Why is the office designed this way? What unspoken rules inform how people engaged on the conference call you joined the other day? Why do your friends post what they do on social media?

Curiosity is not *if* you pay attention. It's *how* you pay attention and where your attention leads you. Before you board for your next trip, here are a few facts about curiosity to take with you.

Everyone Is Curious

Samantha Futerman, a 25-year-old actress in Los Angeles, was preparing for the premiere of her new film, *21 & Over*. Before heading to the red carpet, she was scrolling through her Facebook feed and saw a friend request from someone who looked just like her—I mean *just* like her. It was like seeing a friend request from yourself.

First she thought it was spam. The request came from Anaïs Bordier, a 25-year old French fashion designer living in London. Anaïs messaged Samantha saying, "Hey. My name is Anaïs, I am French and live in London." She invited Samantha to check out her photos and videos and offered key details: She was born in Busan, South Korea, on November 19, 1987. And she was adopted. She ended her message with "Don't freak out… . Lots of love, Anaïs."

Samantha was stunned. She was also born in Busan, South Korea, on November 19, 1987. She was always curious about her past. "As an adoptee," Samantha says, "You have to be open to new expectations and new opportunities."

As Samantha looked through Anaïs's Facebook page, she couldn't believe how much they looked alike. They had similar tastes and enjoyed similar activities. She says, "I accepted her friend request because … it was all too crazy to not be true. I was pretty excited, like, omigod, this could be my twin."[2]

Anaïs and Samantha followed their curiosity to connect, met each other, and had their DNA tested to confirm they were twins. Eventually they traveled together back to Korea. While in South Korea, both girls discovered they shared a sense of curiosity, not only in wanting to track down their birth mother but also to explore the culture they left as infants. Are Samantha and Anaïs both curious because they're twins? Or is it a coincidence?

Researchers love to study identical twins because they're the best way to find out what's genetic versus what's learned from how we're brought up. Geneticist Beben Benyamin led a massive study that reviewed almost every twin study from the last fifty years, involving more than 14.5 million twin pairs. The results show that nature and nurture are almost tied when it comes to traits like curiosity.[3] Anaïs and Samantha were born curious. And their respective families and schools influenced the way they pursue their curiosity. The same is true for you and me.

Everyone is curious. And your brain loves curiosity. When your curiosity is piqued, your brain becomes a magnetic force sucking in whatever new and interesting information it can find. Curiosity drives learning and retention because it changes the chemical makeup of your brain.

A group of neuroscientists from the University of California-Davis used functional magnetic resonance imaging (fMRI) scans to look at the brain's activity when subjects were presented with a series of questions. Interesting questions flood the brain with dopamine, the brain's pleasure drug. Dopamine functions as a neurotransmitter in the brain. Most rewards, such as food, sex, and drugs, all increase the level of dopamine in the brain. Just before an orgasm, dopamine levels are at their peak. When we actively pursue new information through our curiosity, we're rewarded with a similar flood of dopamine. In addition, the researchers found that curious minds show increased activity in the hippocampus, which is involved in the creation of memories. In fact, the degree to which the hippocampus and reward pathways interact predicts an individual's ability to remember other seemingly irrelevant and boring information.[4]

You and I were born curious. But we don't all use curiosity equally. I'm going to teach you how to harness your curiosity to see the world in a way that most travelers miss. Curiosity is one of the most important, defining characteristics of what it means to be human. And applying curiosity to travel is one of the best ways to use it. It just takes a little effort and practice to leverage its power for you.[5]

Benefits of Curiosity

Curiosity yields a long list of benefits, a few of which are worth reviewing before your next trip. Robots will never match what a curious human is capable of doing. Nurturing your curiosity can make you smarter, help you solve problems, and make you happier. It's a key to any good relationship and helps you stay safe, save money, and connect with locals when you travel.

Curiosity Keeps Us Alive

It's tempting to view the twenty-first-century world as the pinnacle of innovation, from space travel to robots, to ever improving technology. But look back several hundred years and consider how curiosity was built into our ancestors' way of life. There were no YouTube videos to teach you how to hunt your dinner or make your berries last through winter. Through trial and error, you figured it out. For most of civilization, our collective curiosity was oriented around meeting the basic needs of food, clothing, and shelter.

But our ancestors' curiosity didn't stop with meeting their basic needs. It expanded to the development of faith systems, literature, arts, cuisine, technology, and so much more. Just look at the development of irrigation systems globally. What began as simply a responsible use and conservation of water soon developed into a mesmerizing irrigation system built across places as far apart as Egypt, Mesopotamia, and Southeast Asia.

Our minds are always looking for ways to improve and innovate. Curiosity is so important to a healthy mind that without it, brain tissue gets destroyed.[6] In fact, when malevolent leaders try to brainwash people, they restrict all forms of outside information, so that the information being used to brainwash them seems all the more stimulating and engaging.[7] So curiosity is more than just a nice to have. Our physical and mental survival depends on it.

Where will your curiosity take you? Follow it. It's good for your brain, and it's good for the world! We can't survive without it.

Curiosity Fuels Our Learning

Albert Einstein famously said, "I have no special talent. I am only passionately curious." There's little you can't learn to do with the combination of devoted attention and curiosity. Do talent and IQ matter? Sure. But innate talent pales in contrast to curiosity and perseverance.

There's mounting evidence that being "smart" is only half as important to your success as your quest and drive to learn. Angela Duckworth's research on grit finds that effort counts twice as much as talent. And the first characteristic shared by all the gritty is that they're driven by an interest and curiosity in the task or skill they're pursuing.[8]

A similar line of thought has emerged from Carol Dweck's groundbreaking work on the growth mindset, a belief that one can grow and develop through dedication, hard work, and curiosity. Dweck argues against categorizing people as smart and talented and provides compelling evidence that curiosity and openness help us push through barriers when we get stuck. Curiosity will help you push ahead for Plan B when you don't get into your dream school or get offered the position you really wanted. The key lies in determining strategies that allow you to get through an impasse—an active learning approach powered by curiosity.[9] Travel is the ideal way to do this, and we'll explore several examples in the chapters ahead.

Curiosity Makes Us Happy

If all that isn't enough, curiosity makes you happy. Most of us won't turn down a chance to be happier. The majority of adults spend less than 20 percent of their day doing things that make them happy.[10] The typical day for most people is spent working at an unfulfilling job, commuting to and from that job, taking care of mundane responsibilities like laundry, fixing things that are broken, standing in line, getting meals, and then at last— chilling out. And how do most people chill out after a boring, unfulfilling day? By watching TV, snacking, or scrolling through their social media feed to see the amazing things all their friends appear to have been doing all day.

It doesn't have to be this way. For a species that built irrigation systems across the globe and traveled to space, surely our curious brains can help us live happier lives. The two keys for having a fulfilling life are the ability to count on someone for help and learning something new yesterday.[11] When you learn to practice your innate curiosity, even the mundane can become interesting.

Discovering new things makes us happy. Look for elements of surprise in your day. Harvard psychologist Daniel Gilbert discovered that we're less likely to find joy in things we plan and more likely to find joy in unexpected experiences we stumble upon.[12] Several of our family's most engaging, joy-filled experiences from our global expeditions have come by surprise. Walking the streets of a new place, roaming the aisles of a grocery store, and stopping to try the local snacks being sold wherever we are is often far more entertaining to us than the big, must-see sites are. It's harder to be surprised at home while going about day-to-day life, but you can strive to replicate some of the same sense of exploration. By cultivating curiosity and remaining open to new experiences, we increase our likelihood of stumbling on interesting, surprising, and satisfying activities.

Curiosity Squashes Stereotypes

Curiosity is one of the best ways to squash stereotypes. Rather than making the lazy assumption that all Millennials or all Chinese or all police officers are the same, curiosity promotes a quest to understand before rushing to conclusions.

What happens when you experience an inexplicable behavior? The curious resist filling in the blanks by using a stereotype and instead think, *Hmm ... I need to learn more.*

Think about a cultural group that is difficult for you to relate to. It might be someone from the other side of the world, or it just as likely might be a group from your own hometown that has an ideological or political mindset different from yours. Curiosity means you resist lazily filling in the blanks and instead genuinely seek to see the world through another's eyes. Consider others' perspective, how they arrived at it, and what you can learn from it.

Curiosity is linked to several other positive outcomes. For example, when you're in the middle of a dispute or negotiation, resolution is impossible without curiosity. If you become defensive and are unwilling to listen to the other person's point of view, then you are not exercising curiosity and have clogged the cognitive process. If you can approach a disagreement from a place of true curiosity, defenses are disarmed, and productive conversations become possible. Curiosity plays a critical role in empathy and strengthens relationships.

How to Spark Curiosity

What can we do to cultivate curiosity in ourselves and others? Most of this book highlights specific ways travel can be used to induce curiosity and leverage its power. But beneath the many travel-oriented examples throughout the book are two key, science-based insights behind what piques curiosity.

Connect the Dots

First, our minds want to close information gaps. Think of the two-year-old who asks *Why, Why, Why?* and you get a glimpse into our quest to connect the dots. Some of the most popular Internet searches are *Why do guys have nipples? Are aliens real?* and *When will I die?* The desire to fill in the blanks drives us. From reading celebrity gossip, to looking online to see what our symptoms mean, traveling to new places, solving crossword puzzles, discovering nuclear physics, and figuring out what happens after we die, we're insatiably curious. It's hardwired into us. We crave knowing, even if there is no obvious benefit. We wonder things like, *Why did their marriage end? How much money does he make? What is that actor like in real life?*

Our lifelong curiosity and playfulness are tied to something psychologists call *neoteny*—the retention of childlike characteristics. It's one way we're different from all other mammals. We retain our kidlike curiosity and capacity to learn. Neoteny has worked well for our species. Retaining our childlike interest in learning means we can pick up new ways of doing things and new ways of thinking, which allows us to adapt to new circumstances.

While curiosity is built into who we are as humans, many people lose the quest to improve and innovate and get in a rut. The curious traveler works against that temptation by continuing the quest to learn and discover. And when asked a question, curious travelers aren't afraid to admit when they don't have an answer because it's more important for them to learn than to look smart.

Albert Einstein said, "The important thing is not to stop questioning. Curiosity has its own reason for existing." If you want to spark curiosity in yourself or others, find an information gap.

Manage Uncertainty

The other way to pique curiosity is through uncertainty. Our brains and bodies have a love/hate relationship with uncertainty. If we experience too much uncertainty, we get anxious. And if we're too anxious, we're unlikely to curiously explore. Anxiety results in an increased heart rate and blood pressure, tightening of the stomach, and perspiration. Our muscles move into threat mode rather than being in a relaxed state, and we're distracted from taking in what's going on around us.[13] But with too little uncertainty, we become bored and disengaged and may feel little motivation to explore. We're most comfortable when things are certain, but we feel most alive when they aren't.

Todd Kashdan, one of the foremost contemporary researchers on curiosity, describes curiosity and uncertainty as two knobs on a radio: anxiety and exploration.[14] When you're anxious, don't try turning down the "anxiety knob." Instead, turn up the "exploration knob."

Consider it this way. If you're upset because you miss a flight, it does little good for someone to say, "Calm down." It's infuriating and makes you more upset. Turning down the anxiety knob rarely works. However, turning up the exploration knob can help in the midst of anxiety. This allows the anxiety to be channeled toward finding a solution or a different way forward. The goal isn't to be less anxious. It's to be alive and reclaim moments so that you build larger behavior patterns aligned with your values.[15]

The next time you're lost in a foreign city, instead of panicking, turn up the exploration knob and note the unexpected places as compared to where you intended to be. Turn finding your way back into a game as a way to motivate you to get back and to avoid getting trapped by the fear of anxiety.

Curiosity and anxiety live in tension with each other in our brains. And travel taps this reality perfectly. If we have too much anxiety, we won't explore. If anxiety overwhelms our curiosity system, dictating what we do, our plans get hijacked. But with too little anxiety, not only are we bored, but we may engage in unsafe behavior. Therefore, uncertainty fuels curiosity, as long as it's not too overwhelming.

Calling All Curiosity Seekers

You were born curious. It's hardwired into you, and it's an important part of keeping you alive and giving your life meaning. But curiosity often gets stifled as we go about the many responsibilities of life. We need to cultivate it, channel it in the right direction, and practice using it. Use information gaps and uncertainty to fuel curiosity in yourself and others.

The benefits of curiosity go far beyond travel. But travel is the ideal laboratory for practicing and using your curiosity. I'm going to teach you how to channel your innate curiosity as you travel to gain insights about yourself and others.

Explore. Ask questions. Learn. Follow your curiosity. Look around you and consider, *Hmm ... I wonder why that is.* Together we can solve problems, be happier, and create a better future for ourselves and others.

Curiosity Sparks

1. **Use information gaps to spark curiosity.**
   - Use the power of the Internet, social media, and formal education to spark your curiosity.
   - When you hear someone dismiss an entire group of people as dishonest or lazy, push them for information to prove their point.
   - When you find yourself making a dogmatic statement about all people from the "other" political party, stop and ask whether you know why smart, thoughtful people view that party as a better choice.

2. **Use uncertainty to spark curiosity.**
   - There's a reason why marketers, activists, and political candidates scare people about what will happen if they do or don't do something. Use this judiciously to motivate others to be more curious.
   - When interacting with someone who dismisses cultural insight as a soft skill that means nothing, set up a scenario for them where they would be clueless without some insight into what's going on cross-culturally. Do the same for yourself.
   - Imagine the potential security risks that might happen on your upcoming travel if you're clueless about appropriate ways to interact with a customs official (e.g., will offering a "tip" ensure you get arrested or expedite your movement through passport control?).

2

The Power of Cultural Intelligence

How does Taylor Swift sell out stadiums when stadium bands are on their way out? It's because she sings songs about her life that are relatable to young women across the globe.

What makes Nike so popular? It's because they tie their products to inspirational athletes who are tied to a cause.

Why does Childish Gambino get millions of hits on his videos? It's because he gives language to a young black person's experience with more than words; he uses powerful images and feelings that are provocative and relatable without being preachy.

What does all this have to do with travel? Taylor Swift, Nike, and Childish Gambino demonstrate curiosity. But it's more than that. They channel their curiosity to make a connection with people. That's what we're after with becoming a curious traveler. It's about more than just the adventure of travel. It's about combining curiosity and travel with the skills to relate to people wherever you are in whatever you do. And that brings us to cultural intelligence (CQ). CQ is not the same as IQ or personality. It's a skill set that is specifically relevant for interacting with people from diverse backgrounds. If curiosity is the motivator, CQ is the compass for navigating through your overseas adventures.

There are fascinating people everywhere you go. We are so much the same, yet so different. Curiosity gives you the power to better understand yourself and others. And cultural intelligence gives you the skill to translate your curious insights into powerful ways to relate to people different from you.

Beneath the examples and strategies for becoming a curious traveler lies the research on cultural intelligence. This chapter gives you some background on CQ, and you'll see it continue to function as the foundation for the curious traveler in the chapters that follow. Let's start with an overview of CQ, followed by some ways we can apply it to our travel.

CQ: It's a Mindset

What have Taylor Swift and Childish Gambino figured out that others miss? They know how to make their work and ideas relatable to a diverse group of people.

Cultural intelligence helps you improve the way you relate to other people. It's not so much memorizing facts about different groups of people. It's far more relational and dynamic than that. Instead, CQ is a mental framework that equips you to read a situation, predict the outcome, and adapt your thinking and behavior to improve the way you relate. In fact, our research confirms that knowing a lot of facts about a culture doesn't really make you culturally intelligent. Human interactions and travel are far too complex to be reduced to lists about how whole groups of people supposedly act. Besides, most of the situations we face when we travel come with little warning, and there isn't time to reference an oversimplified list of "dos and don'ts." With cultural intelligence, you have a tool to broaden the way you work with and relate to a more diverse group of people.

Twenty years of research reveals four capabilities that consistently describe the culturally intelligent[1]. Businesses around the world invest a lot of time and money to train their teams in CQ but let me just give you a quick, insider introduction to these capabilities and how they relate to the curious traveler.

1. *CQ Drive:* **The interest, confidence, and perseverance to adapt interculturally**

   CQ Drive is just that—it's the driver that keeps us going when we travel. This capability offers the most direct link to curiosity. It's being genuinely curious about others and their cultures. Traveling is emotional. We get angry, excited, frustrated, happy, annoyed, tired, scared, and embarrassed. The curious traveler pays attention to their motivation and energy as they travel.

2. *CQ Knowledge:* **Understanding intercultural norms and differences**

   CQ Knowledge is understanding the values, attitudes, and behaviors of the cultures you encounter as you travel. Rather than memorizing facts or the dos and don'ts of a culture, the culturally intelligent look for contrasts in how a culture communicates, deals with conflict, and respects its elders. In today's information age, this is more about taking the responsibility to curiously gather the information most relevant to your situation in the moment than mastering vast amounts of data.

3. *CQ Strategy:* **Making sense of culturally diverse experiences and planning accordingly**

   CQ Strategy is the ability to make sense of what you experience and observe as you travel. It means continuing to push beneath the surface in yourself and others. It's checking your assumptions, reflecting on what you're learning, and going beyond the superficial stereotypes to dig deeper. Most of the strategies and tips shared throughout the book—suspend judgment, consider whether there's another explanation, check your assumptions—stem from the research behind this capability we call CQ Strategy.

4. *CQ Action:* **Changing verbal and nonverbal actions appropriately when interacting interculturally**

   CQ Action is demonstrating the behavioral flexibility to suit the cultural differences you encounter as you travel. The culturally intelligent are not chameleons who appropriate the behaviors of whatever culture they encounter. But they understand the need to adapt to be effective and respectful. Curiosity helps you observe the different verbal and nonverbal behaviors like greetings, gift giving, feedback, and compliments, so that when appropriate, you can flex your action to mirror those behaviors.

There are a number of promising benefits for culturally intelligent travelers. CQ is proven to predict your adjustment to a new cultural environment, decision-making, cost savings, safety, innovation, and the list continues. Employers are not just looking for experienced candidates; they want individuals who are equipped to work effectively with people from all kinds of backgrounds. CQ not only prepares you for travel but for your life journey.

CQ doesn't develop in a straight line. There are moments when we are successful at slowing down to improve how we relate, and others when we're exhausted or irritated and abort the culturally intelligent mindset. But the more you focus on cultivating a CQ mindset, the more it will become part of you. And that not only applies to travel; it relates to people anywhere and everywhere. Part of how Donald Glover went from an unknown comedy writer to the wildly famous Childish Gambino was his ability to channel his curiosity to create relatable comedy and music. He has this fascinating ability to use soul music, television, and comedy to make art that is politically substantive without becoming preachy, and that sounds a whole lot like CQ.[2]

Expert Snapshots

Let's get more specific. What does it look like to apply CQ and curiosity to travel? Let me take you a world away from pop culture and spring break trips for a few minutes to learn how the experts apply CQ to studying another culture. When anthropologists study a culture, the real magic comes from visiting the culture and experiencing it firsthand. There's something different about the way an anthropologist travels and interacts with people compared to what you see through your favorite Instagram influencer's selfies.[3] These are things all of us can do if we put our minds to it.

An Amazon Tribe

Napoleon Chagnon, one of the foremost contemporary anthropologists, devoted thirty-five years of his career to living in the jungle with the Yanomamö people. The Yanomamö tribe is a group of about 35,000 indigenous people who live in in the Amazon rainforest; they are the most isolated tribal group in the Americas. Many villages have still never encountered any outsiders.

When Chagnon arrived, he expected to find what eighteenth-century philosopher Jean Jacques Rousseau called "noble savages"—primitive people living peacefully in a pristine state of nature. Chagnon had been taught that indigenous peoples live peacefully when they haven't been corrupted by outside influences like colonizers or missionaries. He expected to meet a tribe that would welcome him and take him in as their own.

These idealistic notions were quickly shattered for Chagnon. When he arrived at a Yanomamö village for the first time, his first sight was a group of men blowing a green powder up each other's noses through yard-long hollow tubes. Chagnon kept his distance but observed the ritual with great interest. The green powder was blown with such force into the other guy's nose that it came out the other nostril. None of the Yanomamö men approached Chagnon for several minutes, but he could tell they were eyeing him. They hissed, clucked, hooted, screamed, and eventually insisted that he remove the "skins" from his feet. They wanted him to take off his shoes, something they had never seen before, to see if his feet looked like theirs.[4]

Within days of living in the village, a jaguar nearly mauled Chagnon and an anaconda lunged at him from a stream where he went to get a drink. He had to continually rid his hammock of hairy black spiders and rats, but the greatest threat to him was from the Yanomamö who tried to smash his skull with an ax while he slept.[5] This was not what the textbooks said would happen when you visit an indigenous tribe. But Chagnon held his expectations and assumptions loosely.

Chagnon's wife and children eventually joined him. The women touched his wife from head to toe. They marveled at her fair complexion and ran their hands under her blouse to make sure she had breasts. They also ran their hands all over the kids' bodies and kept screeching when they looked at their blond hair.[6]

Curiosity isn't a one-way street. When you visit a place, the locals who live there experience you and your presence just as much and maybe more as you experience theirs.

Chagnon discovered a violent society that looked little like the innocent, pacifist tribal peoples he had studied in his coursework. Warfare permeated all aspects of Yanomamö life and not just between tribes. In fact, Yanomamö men were more often killed by a fellow Yanomamö man than by an outsider. Many anthropologists accused Chagnon of exaggerating his observations, but he never gave up the curious pursuit to understand the people he was studying.

Whenever you encounter an unfamiliar culture, you're susceptible to confirmation bias—the tendency to look for data to confirm your preconceived notions. I've spent a number of years researching the experiences and insights of global travelers. One of my earliest studies looked at the assumptions and insights of charitable volunteers who go into under resourced communities to serve. The majority of volunteers had a shared set of assumptions as they traveled, including the following:

"Poor people are so happy."

"These people have never seen white people before."

"We changed their lives."

A closer look at the communities they served reveals these statements just aren't true. Many of the people are not happy or at least not any happier than people elsewhere. Rare are the places a charitable group goes where the locals have never seen a foreigner. And evidence of lasting change from these kinds of endeavors is difficult to prove. It takes curiosity and CQ to see what is truly going on in the places you visit rather than running on autopilot and seeing what you want to see. Many of these assumptions were things volunteers heard from others who traveled so they went in looking for evidence to confirm their assumptions. The culturally intelligent traveler is aware of their biases going into a new environment. They are open to being surprised, challenged, and even changing their minds.

House Parties

Today, an anthropologist is far more likely to be working for Microsoft or the US government than heading off to the Amazon. Anthropologists are hired to understand what makes people tick.

Min Lieskovsky is a young anthropologist whose recent assignment was commissioned by vodka giant Absolut. Lieskovsky was tasked with studying the elusive phenomenon known as the house party.

At the time, Lieskovsky was a 31-year-old New Yorker who recently left her PhD program at Yale. Her assignment was to attend a variety of house parties where guests bring their favorite vodka and hang out together. She was tasked with studying what went on at these parties and to see what, when, and how people drank. Although her travels were closer to home, there's something to be learned from how she curiously investigated the subculture of house parties with cultural intelligence.

Similar to Chagnon's encounter with the Yanomamö, Lieskovsky watched her subjects with a practiced eye, noting everything she could while also mingling freely with the group. While Chagnon slipped away to his hut in the jungle to scribble notes, Lieskovsky ducked into a bathroom to write down her observations. She noted when the party got started and when it reached its peak, who stuck mustaches on whom, and above all, how the guests interacted with the alcohol. She didn't interpret or evaluate what she observed. She merely described it. She traveled from one house party to the next in order to write an extended description of the rules and rituals—spoken and unspoken—that govern Americans' house parties and, by extension, vodka-buying habits.[7]

Lieskovsky's anthropological task was to figure out what was driving the drinking habits at these vodka house parties. Were they trying to perfect the ideal cocktail? Was it more about the status represented by their choice of alcohol? Or was it mostly about using the alcohol as a social lubricant for having fun?

Absolut assumed buyers of a premium vodka wanted high-end cocktails. The vodka giant prided itself on achieving chemistry-lab purity to create the best vodka in the world. They assumed this was what bonded the people attending the house parties, similar to a group of foodies who seek out the best tapas they can find.

But Lieskovsky discovered something different. Each guest brought a bottle of spirits to the party that eventually ended up on a table overflowing with booze. There was no rhyme or reason to the brands and types strewn across the table. Premium spirits were sitting next to bottom-shelf brands. What mattered most to the partygoers were the stories that accompanied the drinks. Lieskovsky said, "One after another, you see the same thing. Someone comes with a bottle. She gives it to the host, then the host puts it in the freezer and listens to the story of where the bottle came from, and why it's important."[8] It mattered little whether the alcohol was the purist version. What mattered were the stories and bonds associated with the alcohol.

The findings held true as Lieskovsky traveled to house parties in other parts of the country. People were interested in one another's stories about how a product played a role in some memorable event—humorous, self-deprecating stories about first encountering a vodka or discovering a liqueur while traveling in Costa Rica or Mexico. It's not like Lieskovsky had never been to a party. She could have been annoyed by the assignment or defaulted to her assumptions about the kind of people who show up at one of these parties. But she suspended judgment and tried to simply understand.

The real discoveries of travel require looking beyond your expectations, even when traveling into cultures close to home. Like an anthropologist, take in the experiences without judgment and notice what you learn about yourself and others.

Smartphones

The final expert snapshot comes from Sherry Turkle, one of the foremost social scientists studying the impact of technology. Turkle studied the relationship between adolescents and their smartphones. She didn't travel far to do this, but she entered a culture far removed from her world as a seasoned academic at MIT.

Teenagers and college students tell Turkle that the most commonly heard phrase when hanging out with their friends is, "Wait, what?" Everyone phubs—the skill of maintaining eye contact while texting—when hanging out together. It's difficult to keep up with the conversation around you when you're toggling between texts, finding a GIF to send someone, and simultaneously tuning in and out of the people talking around you. Cameron, a college junior, tells Turkle about being out with a group of friends the other night and sending a text to his buddy sitting next to him just to get his attention.[9]

Turkle gets students talking about things that many researchers, much less parents, have a hard time pulling off. Students seem to find solace in talking about their observations and behaviors related to their phones. Researchers wrestle with the ethical dilemma of knowing when to interject their opinions as they interact with their subjects and when to simply observe without judgment. That dilemma is evident in Turkle's work and is something faced by the curious traveler.

One sixteen-year-old says his mother was appalled that he responded to news from his friend that his dad had just died by sending a text. "Why didn't you call him?" his mother asked. "You responded with a text to his dad dying?" Her son defended himself. "It isn't my place to interrupt him. A phone call would be way too intrusive right now."[10] Turkle asked other students what they thought, and without fail, they backed the sixteen-year-old 100 percent. Calling someone is intrusive, particularly in a time of crisis. You should begin by texting.

Where do these rituals get decided? How are they reinforced?

As part of Turkle's ongoing observation, she began to see that students follow the rule of three. When you're with a group at dinner, you check that at least three people have their heads up from their phones before you give yourself permission to look at your phone. As Turkle sat down with a group of eight students, she noticed that as the students talked, their heads were constantly going down to check their phones. A few tried not to, but it's a struggle.

Turkle wasn't interviewing students to judge their use of technology. She's quick to assert that there is nothing wrong with making the most of technology, and she texts her own adult daughter every day. But she also doesn't sit with her scientific discoveries as a neutral observer. She becomes concerned by what she observes and begins to believe that personal conversations are becoming increasingly challenging for a culture that is most comfortable communicating via gifs, social media, and texts. Mounting research reports a 40 percent drop in empathy among college students over the past twenty years, and Turkle has a hunch this is related to the surge in technology use.[11]

Researchers and travelers need to be cautious about asserting cause and effect. But Turkle pays careful attention to the potential influence on kids of growing up in homes where their parents don't get through a meal without stopping to read and respond to a text. Watch for patterns of behavior as you travel and explore potential connections. Talk with locals and find ways to interject your opinion but don't be too quick to do so. Then step away and reflect on what you have observed; see what you learn about yourself and others.

CQ Tools for Curious Travelers

Curiosity is great. But its real power comes when combined with CQ. You likely picked up on several takeaways from how the experts do this. But let me highlight a few key points we can learn from how these researchers combine curiosity with CQ when encountering a new culture.

Get Personal (CQ Drive)

It's impossible to understand a culture at arm's length. You have to find ways to get up close and personal. If you're just traveling somewhere for a week to ten days, getting personal might mean finding ways to engage with other people on the train or a local café. For study abroad students or volunteers staying somewhere for several weeks, it means busting out of the bubble of other visitors from your country and figuring out how to be with locals.

The objective for the culturally intelligent, curious traveler is not simply the adventure of a new place. It's directing the attention of your curiosity toward the people who live there. *How do people here live? What keeps them awake at night? What are their dreams?*

We get some cues about how to get personal by seeing how anthropologists interact with the people they are studying. Most researchers purposely avoid getting personal with their subjects because it clouds objectivity. But you can't follow your curiosity very far if all you have are numbers and secondhand findings. Chagnon knew the only way to really understand the Yanomamö people was to live with them. Turkle knew she needed to sit with adolescents in their preferred environments if she was going to gather accurate insights.

In research, we talk about big data and thick data. Big data are massive quantitative findings that capture key statistical insights. To be useful, big data need to be standardized, normed, defined, and clustered. Big data are all the rage these days. The company with the most big data wins. Or so we're told. Thick data comes from a much smaller sample size because it takes a lot longer to collect. This is the kind collected by Chagnon, Lieskovsky, and Turkle, and it provides discoveries that only come through extended firsthand observation of people's emotions, stories, and worldviews. It's the insights that are tough to quantify.

Tricia Wang tried to get Nokia leadership to pay attention to thick data when she was working for them in 2009. As Wang traveled across China, she had numerous conversations with people along the way. She began to see that low-budget consumers wanted a smartphone, but this went against the millions of data points Nokia leadership had collected that said smartphones wouldn't work in emerging markets. Nokia leadership dismissed Wang's ideas. We all know how that turned out. A few years later Nokia went from owning over 50 percent of the cell phone market to 3 percent.

Use a thick data approach as you embark on your next trip overseas. Linger longer in the same place for a few days to gain an emerging picture of how people think, live, and relate. It's tough to get the most from travel if you only visit tourist attractions and see how many cities you can fit into one trip. I love to stay in residential areas when I travel so I can see what people do in the morning, what kinds of conversations they have at the corner café, and the changes that occur on a weekend as compared to weekdays.

Ask Questions (CQ Knowledge)

Throughout the book, you won't hear me tell you to read everything you can about a culture before you visit. Learning some basic insights is great, but beyond that, the best way to understand a culture is by asking good questions while you're there. Researchers know they can't just directly ask what they're trying to discover. They have to approach issues indirectly. For example, Turkle couldn't just ask teenagers, "Do you have empathy?" She had to figure out what kinds of questions would help her gain insights into their level of empathy. From a research perspective, there's a need to ask the same questions in the same order to multiple individuals. There's no need for you to be that rigid as you travel, but find a question you like and ask different people you meet.

A word of caution here. Questions and curiosity have to be used carefully as you travel because a question asked the wrong way or to the wrong individual can be highly offensive. For example, "why" questions can make people defensive when asked directly so use your CQ to figure out an appropriate way to approach others. I'll show you how as we go through the book.

The basic questions of journalism are a good starting point: who, what, where, when, how, and why? The people you encounter may not have a clue. The questions might just as well be asked of yourself, the answers to which you'll gain through observation and interaction rather than by explicitly asking them. A few examples of questions to consider are the following. Start by asking these of yourself, and then find ways to gather this information from others.

- Who are the "important" people here? Who has the most status?
- What happens at different times of the day in this neighborhood? What's it like here in the morning? Late at night? How does that compare with where I live?
- How does this place look, sound, and smell compared to other places I've been? Before you're too quick to look for similarities, spend as much time paying attention to differences.
- What catches my attention? One of the best parts about being in a different culture is that we tend to notice things with which we aren't familiar. What seems unusual or different?
- How am I viewed here? Am I perceived as an "insider" or "outsider"? How does the perception of me influence my experience here?

- Is there a lot of insider knowledge, or are things made explicit for outsiders?

As you observe a new place with a spirit of curiosity, you begin to move from these preliminary questions to larger questions about how the behaviors, values, and beliefs of people are shaped.

Test Assumptions (CQ Strategy)

When Taylor Swift released her album *Reputation*, she included a personal letter to her fans. She writes, "Here's something I've learned about people... We think we know someone, but the truth is that we only know the version of them they have chosen to show us."[12]

Being aware of how people present themselves is one of the most important CQ tools we need to apply to curious travel. We only know what we can observe. And when we're observing people in a different culture, we might see behaviors that mean something different than we guess. As we move through the traveling dilemmas in Part II, we'll reflect on a group's ideal, observed, and believed behavior. What people say they value is often inconsistent with what their behavior says. Most of the students Turkle interacted with described a high value for conversation and hanging out with friends. But when observing students' actual behavior, they seemed more connected to the friends who weren't with them than those in their presence.

Ideal behavior is how we think we should behave and the image we strive to project to others (think social media!). Think about responding to a survey where someone asks how many times you exercise in a week. If you want to project yourself as someone who is active and fit, you may give what you think is the ideal answer: "I work out at least five times a week."

Observed behavior is what others see in how we behave. Through direct observation of your behavior over a week, we can see how much you actually exercise. Of course if you know you're being observed, that may change how you behave.

Believed behavior is how we think we behave in reality (as compared to what we project to others). You might qualify your exercise habits to a friend and say, "It's usually more like three times a week."

Whether observing how people treat deadlines or examining their view of immigrants, pay attention to their *espoused* versus *actual* behavior. Be aware of how your assumptions influence what you see as you travel. Testing assumptions and suspending judgment is one of the most important CQ tools we use throughout the book so I want to give you a few specific guidelines you can apply to your travel.

Before

- Identify your preconceived assumptions and biases upfront. Write them down before you go and discuss them with your fellow travelers.
  ◦ I expect this place will be like …
  ◦ Others have told me …
  ◦ I think I'm going to struggle most with …

During

- Describe what you observe without interpreting it (e.g., people put Smirnoff on the table next to Skyy; people greet you when they enter the elevator). Write it down and/or discuss it with a travel partner.
- Examine the same situation in multiple contexts (e.g., the morning commute in different places you visit).
- Beware of assuming "cause and effect" (e.g., don't assume that what you observe leads to something else you observe).

After

- Compare your observations with what research states about this phenomenon or issue. Or check with someone who has a lot of experience and insight with the culture.

Talk to people as you travel. Ask what they enjoy doing. Discuss with them the priority of academics, family, career, sports, and more. I would even say, find moments to tackle the untouchable subjects of politics and religion. See how what you observe in the actual behaviors, advertisements, and events around you align with those conversations.

Be Yourself, Sort of (CQ Action)

When you look at people like Taylor Swift, Napoleon Chagnon, and Childish Gambino, you see people who are comfortable in their own skin. They have an uncanny ability to use their curiosity and CQ to understand and relate to people different from them, but they don't overdo it.

The culturally intelligent traveler is flexible without over adapting. Chagnon and Turkle weren't quick to judge, but neither did they remain neutral. They took time to curiously understand the values and behaviors of the cultures they encountered and when necessary formed a value judgment for themselves.

Some of the traveling dilemmas in the next section will strike at the core of your values and beliefs. I'm not asking you to travel the world with a manila curiosity that views all behavior as ethically relative or equal. But I am asking us to slow down before being too quick to judge different as weird or wrong.

Curiosity X CQ = Global Citizen

It's easy to walk through an airport or move from one city to the next without really seeing the people there—fellow travelers, locals, airport staff. Cultural intelligence allows you to make a connection. And when you direct curiosity with CQ, you not only observe the similarities and differences of the places you go, but you *see* people and connect with them.

 You were born curious. We get different amounts of the trait genetically, but we're all curious. However, curiosity is a voluntary muscle. If you don't use it, it begins to atrophy. You get in a rut and fail to be surprised by the wonder around you. But with a little practice, you can fire it up and experience its benefits wherever you go.

No one is born culturally intelligent. CQ is a learned skill that allows you to direct your curiosity to make connections with people from different backgrounds. CQ gives you a lens that directs your curiosity to see differences, understand them, and respond to them respectfully and effectively.

 Research proves that curiosity x CQ ensures your travel is an investment that keeps paying dividends. CQ is a force multiplier. It allows you to plan a trip that will have more lasting value and help you with many practical situations along the way. Curiosity x CQ is the pathway toward being a global citizen, and it has the power to transform your career and relationships.

Now the real fun begins as we dive into a series of dilemmas you're sure to face as you travel with curiosity near and far.

To learn more about cultural intelligence:
- Visit culturalq.com where you'll find CQ articles, videos, and assessments.
- Read *Leading with Cultural Intelligence.*

Part II
Traveling Dilemmas

One of the reasons curiosity and travel fit so well together is travel inevitably brings you face to face with a number of confounding dilemmas. Some of them are small—*Why don't they just post a sign telling you what time they open?* Other observations bring you face to face with ethical and moral dilemmas—*How can a contemporary society defend treating women that way?* There is no end to the dilemmas I've encountered through travel. And even though I've been doing this for thirty years, I still come across dilemmas that leave me confused and sometimes irritated.

I've selected five dilemmas that consistently come up as I'm talking to fellow travelers. I'm not going to tell you how to solve the dilemmas per se. That's not really the point. Instead, I want to pique your curiosity by describing some of the issues related to these dilemmas and suggest what it looks like to respond to these kinds of situations with cultural intelligence and curiosity.

Each chapter concludes with a list of Curiosity Challenges related to the dilemma. But the real discoveries are in the stories and your reflections as you consider these situations. As you read them, write down dilemmas of your own and see what you can learn from applying curiosity to them.

> Several of the dilemmas reflect key differences in values between cultures. See the appendix for a list of ten cultural values and ways they influence work and relationships.

3
DILEMMA: WHERE'S THE QUEUE?

I was boarding a flight in Bangkok, and my North American colleague said, "Asians are so deferential until they board a bus or plane. Then they push, shove, and elbow you out of the way. What's up with that?"

What *is* up with that? Following the rules to wait your turn in line is a big deal to a lot of travelers—and not so much to others.

Americans wait in line for all kinds of things, from renewing a driver's license and queueing up at the supermarket to waiting to board a flight. We're forever looking for ways to speed up long, boring waits though some actually seem to enjoy the cultic energy that comes from waiting in line for hours to get the new iPhone or Black Friday special. Others pay extra money to avoid long lines at amusement parks. For most people across the United States, waiting your turn is an unspoken social contract.

Try boarding a train in India and you'll know you've entered a world that plays by a different set of rules. Before an inbound train even stops, many passengers push to get off first while others are simultaneously shoving to get onboard. People have died boarding trains during peak hours. All across India, I've had people butt ahead of me in pretty much any context you can imagine—banks, restaurants, stores, hospitals, and even temples.

Hmm … I wonder why that is.

Are Indians just ruder than Americans? Have they never been taught the polite way to queue up? Or are Americans the rude ones, insisting everyone line up in order, regardless of their status or importance?

Head over to Tokyo and you'll quickly see this dilemma can't be explained as an East versus West difference. The scene in Tokyo train stations couldn't be more different from those in Delhi. Thousands of people in dark suits walk deliberately through the terminal. When you get to the train platforms, people are lined up single-file according to painted lines that inform passengers where to queue up. No one enforces this, people just do it.

Waiting in lines is a huge part of travel, and it's never an activity of choice. But instead of just viewing queues as a necessary evil, use them as a chance to stop and curiously consider what lies behind the different behaviors you encounter. Knowing why Americans, Indians, and Japanese queue the way they do is less important than slowing down from assuming one way of queueing is better than the other. Watching how people queue may be just as enlightening as the museum you're waiting to enter.

School Days

Learning how to form an orderly line was one of the first things I learned in school. Anytime we left the classroom, we had to form a single-file line. Someone was designated as the line leader of the week, and if you became unruly walking the halls or veered from the single-file queue, you were given the ultimate punishment—placement at the back of the line. The message implicitly taught to American children, and British, Singaporean, Japanese, Australian, and many other kids around the world, is that someday, at some point, if you are polite and patient and play by the rules, you will get your turn to be at the front of the line.

What if you grow up going to school in southern Europe or India, places where waiting in orderly lines seems to play much less importance? For the most part, queueing is still part of the early classroom experience. And in fact, teachers in many of these places put far more rigidity around queueing up than what you experience in places like the United States and Sweden. You can find videos online of schoolchildren lining up meticulously in

India, China, and Israel. So why do people from many of these cultures abandon what they learned in school when they queue everywhere else?

Kids who grow up in places like the United States or Japan see orderly queuing reinforced everywhere they go. Their parents line up that way when checking out a book at the library or buying something at the convenience store. In Germany, the social pressure to stand obediently at a crosswalk, even if no traffic is within sight in either direction, ensures that most Germans will wait their turn.

In contrast, even though kids in places like India or Brazil are taught to queue up in school, they implicitly receive a different message elsewhere. A queue is something you do when authority figures make you do it—such as lining up at school, at the bank, or when voting. But when no one is around to enforce the rules, a different sense of order takes over. You fend for yourself when boarding a bus or crossing the street.

Survival

One of the first questions anthropologists consider when entering a new culture is *How do people survive here?* They want to know what mechanisms a society has developed to cope with life and figure out how those norms get passed from one generation to the next.

Pushing and asserting yourself is a necessity in many parts of the world. You will never get on some trains in India if you follow the schoolteacher's mantra, "Everyone will get a turn. Just wait in line." Everyone won't get a turn. Some are going to be left behind, and a certain level of aggressiveness becomes necessary to survive. Delhi journalist Ranjani Iyer Mohanty says, "We live in a hugely-populated, resource-constrained country.... If we wait patiently in a queue, by the time our turn comes up, the item is sold out."[1]

In his novel *Shantaram*, Gregory David Roberts refers to this dilemma as the doctrine of necessity. The amount of force and violence necessary to board a train in India is no less and no more than the amount of politeness and consideration necessary to ensure that the cramped journey is as pleasant as possible. Roberts writes, "If there were a billion Australians or Americans living in such a small space, the fighting to board the train would be much more, and the courtesy afterward much less."[2] In some cases, pushing ahead can be a matter of feeding your family, and if you don't aggressively get to the front of the queue, you're viewed as weak.

A very different method of survival exists in Anglo cultures. The priority of queueing among Westerners is thought to have its origins in the Industrial Revolution. As large groups of people moved from the English countryside to urban settings, patterns of daily life began to change, including a more formalized approach to conducting daily business. Authorities used queues to instill fair play, and waiting your turn to get your bit of rations was a necessity. Anglo cultures began to use lines to ensure decency, fair play, and democracy.[3]

We learn behaviors that increase our chances for survival or success. Once this behavior is formed and becomes the norm, it is passed from generation to generation. Anthropologist Oscar Lewis says, "By the time ... children are age six or seven they have usually absorbed the basic values of their subculture."[4] You're not going to change the way people queue so take a deep breath and see what you can learn from it.

Do You Know Who I Am?

I was getting ready to board a flight headed to Ghana when the gate agent told us the flight had been canceled. We all lined up to make alternative arrangements except for one guy who marched ahead of everyone. He demanded help because of the important meeting he had to attend in Accra. The agent patiently told him that everyone in line had important plans and he would need to wait his turn. He proceeded to tell her how many miles he had flown on the airline and that he expected to be treated accordingly or he'd talk to her supervisor. She told him again that he needed to wait his turn.

I experienced the reverse when I recently flew from Mumbai to Abu Dhabi. I was flying economy class so I got in line to check in at the economy ticket counter. An airline representative walked up to me and said, "Follow me, sir." And just like that, I was escorted to the posh lobby and check-in section for business class passengers.

This hardly sounds like a dilemma, right? I was all too grateful to avoid the long lines winding around to the economy check-in counter. But I felt a bit guilty so I stopped the guy and said, "Actually, sir, I'm flying economy today so I can just check in over there." To which he emphatically responded that this was where I belonged. I was directed through special lines for people "like me" with no one questioning why I was there while holding an economy boarding pass.

First come, first served is the social contract that guides queuing up in places like Canada and Sweden, although even there, implicit bias causes some people to be treated preferentially, or not, based on how they look. But in places like Mumbai and Abu Dhabi, the social contract says, "VIPs served first." Some individuals' time and responsibilities are perceived as more important than others, therefore surely waiting on them should be a priority. I'm no VIP. But I "appeared" important so I was automatically assumed to be worthy of jumping the queue.

In one culture, the privileged wait in line to prove they know the rules of etiquette. In another culture, the privileged are escorted to the front of the line. *Hmm ... I wonder why that is.*

Who Goes First?

While first come, first served is the guiding principle in many cultures and VIPs first is the guiding rule in others, a number of other factors determine who goes first. See if you know which unspoken rules apply to these situations.

Dubai. You and another person ride a lift together. You're both getting off on the same floor. Who goes first?

London. You and a colleague are walking toward a building. Who goes through the door first?

Tokyo. You walk up to a group of Japanese work colleagues. Whom do you greet first? Does it matter?

If you're in the Middle East, the person to the right of the elevator (when facing forward) alights first. In Western cultures, men have traditionally waited for a woman to enter a doorway first. That custom is fading, but at the very least, the first person to get to the door is expected to hold it open for the person behind them. In Japan, you begin by greeting the most senior person in the group, by age and/or authority. Failure to follow these norms can be uncomfortable for everyone.

Hierarchical societies (see the appendix) put authority figures at the front of the line—both as a way to respect their position and to get them on to the important things they need to do. Flight crews go through airport security first in many airports as a way to efficiently get all of us going where we need to go. Most US airlines allow military personnel to board first out of respect for those who serve their country.

The shipping industry has a sorting method called the law of gross tonnage, a convention that says the bigger ship has the right of way. This is similar to what happens among many animals where there's a well-established protocol that the more dominant animal has the right of way.[5] Who goes first is ubiquitously built into culture. You get a sense of what a culture values based on who goes first, which leads me to shopping and driving.

The Zipper Merge

One time I stopped at a supermarket while I was in Saudi Arabia. Supermarkets offer fascinating insight into a culture. I picked up a few items and walked up to the cashier line, staying behind the couple in line ahead of me.

Just as the couple ahead of me finished paying, an elderly woman walked up and placed a carton of milk on the counter in front of me. There's no question I was "next," but the cashier immediately served her. This annoyed me, but I took it in stride, particularly given that the customer was older and I knew this was a part of how life happens here. Then another guy came up from the other side of the counter and started waving his money and a pack of cigarettes. I dropped my items loudly on the counter to make sure the cashier was aware of my presence and frustration. The man with cigarettes said something in Arabic, the cashier took his money, and when I thought for sure I'd be next, another woman walked up and placed a package in the cashier's hand. at which point I said, "Unbelievable!" I shook my head and walked out of the store with my items left behind.

I talked with a Saudi friend about this afterward and asked him why the cashier didn't just serve people in the order we queued. "How many items did you have?" he asked. I told him I had about eight to ten small things. "Ah, that explains it!," he said. "It makes more sense for the cashier to take care of people who only have one or two items first and then help the people with more items after that. Next time, you'll be grateful when you only have two things." *It makes more sense to whom?* I thought.

Isn't it more efficient to use an orderly form of queuing? Doesn't *that* make the most sense?

Take driving as an example. Places like Canada and Japan make it clear where you should be on the road based on which direction you're going. It just makes sense to people from there. Roads are much more fluid in places like India or Egypt where people use whatever space is needed. Larger vehicles usually have the right of way unless a motorcycle or rickshaw finds a way to squeeze through. Which makes the most sense? It depends on where you're from. But is one way more efficient than the other?

In most Western cities, lanes are clearly marked and drivers are given clear instructions about where to drive and how to merge in a construction zone. When two lanes merge into one, road rage occurs if a driver waits until the last minute to force themselves into the single lane of traffic.

Many studies indicate that those "rude" drivers who merge at the last minute are actually helping the overall flow of traffic. They're using the "zipper merge" where more of the roadway is put to use with people taking turns merging into the single lane. Some US states saw such an improvement from the zipper merge that they created campaigns to teach people how to do it. Colorado saw a 15 percent increase in traffic flow after implementing the zipper merge and 50 percent shorter lines.[6] Beware of assuming that one way of queueing is more efficient than the other. Notice the differences as you travel and resist rushing to judgment.

But It's Just Not Logical

The different ways cultures organize groups of people to drive, board a train, or get into a museum help you see that what seems orderly and logical to one person might seem just the opposite to another. These curious reflections around something as simple as queuing can lead to broader insights about the diverse ways our global society thinks and behaves.

Think about it this way. Which two words in each list below most logically belong together?

1. monkey rhinoceros banana
2. oven baking refrigerator
3. uniform police teacher
4. wheat curry rice
5. fish milk water
6. orchestra violin guitar
7. blackboard chalk pencil
8. trains trucks tracks
9. elevator house skyscraper
10. China Beijing Malaysia

Most people tend to organize each group of words either by category (e.g., animals together, cities together) or by relationship (e.g., animal and its food, city and country). What two words did you put together?

Category		Relationship
monkey and rhinoceros	or	monkey and banana
oven and refrigerator	or	oven and baking
police and teacher	or	police and uniform
wheat and rice	or	rice and curry
milk and water	or	fish and water
violin and guitar	or	orchestra and violin
chalk and pencil	or	blackboard and chalk
trains and trucks	or	trains and tracks
China and Malaysia	or	China and Beijing

You may have done some of both—category-based pairs and relationship-based pairs. But most people use one primary approach to grouping the nouns. Western cultures typically highlight the category-based approach where items are grouped around taxonomies and hard boundaries. To the Western mind, this is what seems most logical and orderly. Eastern and southern cultures are more likely to use the relationship-based approach wherein an emphasis on connections and themes is perceived as a more logical, orderly approach.

Waiting in single-file lines fits the category-based approach to life. The person at the front of the line is next to be served. There are different lines for different classes of service or for getting into different attractions. There's no blur or confusion. Most nouns in Western languages reflect sharp boundaries: *apples*, *oranges*, *pencils*, and *pens*. Adjectives are used to allow for some of the blur such as *green* apples or *ripe* apples, but they're still all apples. Something cannot be partially an apple. It is either an apple or it is not. The bud and blossom are not considered "apples." Things are identified based on the category to which they belong. From personality types to taxonomies of plants and animals, categories permeate life in the West. You're either next in line or you aren't.

In the category-based world, order and cleanliness come from keeping things in their place. Forks are placed with forks and knives with knives. The walls of a room are uniform in color, and when a creative shift in color occurs, it usually happens at a corner or along a straight line midway down the wall. Lawns are edged and dandelions are removed with a clear border between the sidewalk and the lawn. Roads have clearly defined lanes, and music is built on a scale with seven distinct notes and five half steps. Each note has a fixed pitch, and a good performance occurs when the musicians hit the notes precisely. Maintaining boundaries is essential in a category-based world, otherwise chaos sets in.[7] Is it any wonder why someone butting ahead in line causes blood pressures to soar?

Most of the world is much less concerned about sharp boundaries and sees things in a more relationship-based way. Categories flow into one another as do lines and the people waiting in them. Day becomes night, and a mountain turns into a plain without a clear distinction between when it stops being a mountain. Even birthdays are treated more ambiguously in some places such as many Asian cultures where a newborn is "one" at the time of birth and gains another year each New Year's holiday.

In relationship-based cultures, different colors of paint may be used at various places on the same wall. And the paint may "spill" over on the window glass, but why should that matter? Meals are a fascinating array of ingredients where food is best enjoyed when mixed together on your plate and everyone shares from communal dishes. Roads are more fluid with traffic using the amount of space needed at the time. People walk along the street bumping into other pedestrians along the way and see little need to apologize. "Queues" for boarding a bus are more of a loosely defined group of people waiting near the bus stop together. When Israeli-born author Ayelet Tsabari first visited Canada she noticed people stood in straight lines at every bus stop. To her, it appeared as if they were commanded by an invisible drill sergeant. She was so perplexed.

The way we queue is deeply built into how we view and organize the world. When you stop to think about how and why people queue the way they do, you suddenly gain a window into many other behaviors that most of us take for granted.

What's Behind a Queue?

There's nothing inherently better about one way of queueing versus another. Nor is there any need for you to feel guilty for the way you prefer to queue. But as you travel, take a deep breath and use the diverse approaches to queues as an opportunity to learn about yourself and others. Something as simple as how people queue can elicit fascinating insights on how a culture operates and what it values.

Curiosity Challenges | Queues

Different approaches to queues is one of the things that annoys travelers most. Curious travelers with CQ work on expanding their comfort zone while waiting in line.

Low CQ and Closed	High CQ and Curious
That's so rude!	I'll try queuing that way.

- Waiting in line is never the activity of choice. But turn it into a cultural experience. See what you can learn about the culture and yourself. Discuss it with your fellow travelers.
- When standing in line, notice who expects to be treated differently. Are there any consistencies?
- See if you can make it through a whole day of queuing up without getting annoyed. Have a competition with your travel partners to see who can last the longest without complaining about the queuing system.
- Notice whether there are any differences in how different age groups or genders queue in the places you visit. Do people queue differently for different contexts (public transit vs. supermarket vs. bank)?
- Pretend you're briefing a new visitor on the queueing norms for where you're visiting. Explain the norms without using any negative language.

4
Dilemma: Do I Eat the Eye?

Food is the curious traveler's drug of choice. What do people eat and why? Is the big meal at 1 PM, 6 PM, or 10 PM? How are you supposed to eat *that*?

Most people in the United States and Europe consider insects a disgusting thing to eat whereas many other people around the world make them a regular part of their diets. Some consider frozen chicken breasts a more sanitary way to buy chicken while others think the one just butchered is a healthier choice. Some cultures like their meat cooked, others like it raw, and still others like it slightly spoiled.

Hmm ... I wonder why that is.

I can't think of a better way to put your curiosity to work when traveling than through food. Food is a central part of what anthropologists study when seeking to understand any culture. What we eat says a lot about who we are and where we're from.

What's Your Comfort Food?

I recently asked my social media network to share their favorite comfort foods. The diversity of responses was mind-boggling. Chicken noodle soup, laksa, feijoada, spaghetti pie, ramen, grilled cheese, tikki, congee, dodo, empanadas, and the list kept going. Many people from the same places listed different foods. Food is both cultural and personal.

Former *New York Times* reporter Jennifer 8. Lee says her go-to comfort food is a plate of kimchi with white rice and fried Spam. In her wildly popular TED Talk, she says that what we eat is an accumulation of our life experiences, including where you grew up, people you've dated, and places you've visited. We often pick up favorite foods from various places we've lived or encountered along the way, but we continue to come back to foods that mean something to us.[1] For most of us, our comfort foods stem from our upbringing. But the curious traveler expands and diversifies the menu of options that bring comfort.

Soon after we arrived in Singapore the first time, my wife wasn't feeling well. She asked me to pick up some saltine crackers and ginger ale. It's what her mom gave her when she got sick, though neither of us really stopped to think about that at the moment. When our Singaporean neighbor learned what Linda was eating to heal her ailing stomach, she was appalled. "Crackers and soda aren't going to do anything for you. I'm going to make you a pot of congee," a rice porridge commonly eaten across Asia for breakfast and especially when you're sick. She insisted there were healing qualities that come from eating porridge. A bowl of soggy rice didn't sound appealing, but Linda agreed to give it a try and actually enjoyed it. What we find comforting is often rooted in what we ate as a child. Ironically, congee is now part of our family's menu of options when someone gets sick.

My comfort foods are both a product of my upbringing and my experiences. The first thing that comes to mind when I think about comfort food is an authentic sweet and spicy Thai curry or a tasty bowl of ramen, likely stemming from the number of years I've spent in Asia. But there's also something very comforting about going home and having my mom's gooey cheese loaf or one of her pasta casseroles. Those foods bring back many comforting memories of my carefree days as a kid. Even kids who didn't grow up in a happy home usually pine for the foods they ate as a child.

I was recently in line at the breakfast buffet at an Asian hotel and a British guy walked up behind me. When he saw the options—noodles, soup, fried rice—he scoffed. "They call this breakfast? I'll eat my dinner tonight, thank you very much, but where's the breakfast food?" I couldn't resist sniping back. "For most of the world, this is breakfast food, but if you can't handle it, there's cereal over there." While many travelers I encounter aren't as rude as this guy, I've often observed a reticence to changing up one's breakfast routine more than other meals. There seems to be a greater willingness to curiously explore different foods at lunch or dinner while sticking to what's familiar for breakfast. I get it. For a long time, the idea of noodles or soup for breakfast just didn't sit well with me. Maybe there's something about having what's familiar first thing in the morning that helps us reset for a new day.

Food Judging

Food is more than just sustenance. We judge people based on what they eat, and those opinions are socialized in us from our cultures.

A group of university students were asked to rate people based on what they eat. The students were shown pictures of individuals whose physical appearance and descriptions were nearly identical. The difference was in their diets.

Students were shown a picture of a student with the following description: "Jennifer is a 21-year-old student. She describes herself as active and physically fit and says she regularly enjoys tennis and running. She is 5'4" tall and weighs 125 pounds. The foods she eats most regularly are fruit, salad, homemade whole wheat bread, chicken, and potatoes."

This was the "good food" profile. Students were then shown a nearly identical profile including a description of someone also fit and active, but the last line was switched to *She regularly eats steak, hamburgers, french fries, doughnuts, and double-fudge ice cream sundaes.*

Without fail, students rated the student in the first category as thinner, active, and more fit than the one who ate the "bad" food. It didn't matter that the facts stated that the students had identical physical characteristics and exercise habits. What they ate caused them to be perceived differently.

Further, the student who ate fruit and salad instead of french fries and ice cream was rated as more feminine and attractive. The student who ate the bad foods was equated with being more masculine and less attractive.[2] "Good" and "bad" are how we often talk about food: "I've been bad today" or "That dessert looks sinful." Other times we say "I'm trying to be good" when foregoing another chocolate chip cookie.

There's little question that a diet of french fries and ice cream sundaes is less healthy than fruit and salad. But the salient finding from the study among students was that we associate good and bad characteristics with people based on what they eat, even if it's an occasional splurge. The foods we eat send a message. You may be perceived as more likeable, attractive, and responsible if the food you eat is perceived as "good."

The status associated with foods is a big thing in China. Taking a guest to a seafood buffet or serving abalone, shark's fin, or bird's nest soup is a way to respect a VIP. In recent years, Western companies like Starbucks and Godiva chocolates are thought to send a powerful message of respect and privilege. Drinking Voss water shows how globally sophisticated you are.

McDonald's has benefited from being viewed globally as a young, hip brand. How else do you explain the fact that 30,000 people waited for hours when the first McDonald's opened in Russia? And McDonald's has been a huge success in Paris of all places but primarily among youth who view it as a cool place to hang out with friends. It's less about the food and more about the status associated with the food.

We eat what those we admire eat. We order food and drinks that we initially find unpleasant but do it just to be part of the crowd. And before we know it, we've acquired a taste for it. Culture and food are directly linked.

Acquired Tastes

Speaking of acquired tastes, is there any accuracy to the urban legend that you need to try something ten to fifteen times before you'll like it? Not if you're a dog. Gerald Zhang-Schmidt, an Austrian researcher, tells the story of his dog who routinely begs for extra-hot chili peppers. As soon as his dog bites into the pepper, he jerks away and spits it out. But a few minutes later he comes back asking for another bite, not liking it any more the next time. Repeated exposure to the undesirable food doesn't seem to help dogs acquire a taste for it.

In contrast, our taste as humans evolves. Most people aren't initially any more enthused about the burning sensation of a chili pepper than a dog is, yet many of us gradually grow to like it. Most people who keep trying spicy food eventually get used to the sensation and come to the point of craving something spicy.

Acquired tastes stem in part from the status and social nature attributed to eating. You eat things other people around you eat. Give a baby a sip of coffee or yerba mate or feed them a bite of Brussels sprouts or bitter melon and they instinctively spit it out. Much like a dog, they're initially repulsed by the taste. Go out with friends for sushi, and the novice might start with a roll that doesn't have any raw fish. But before you know it, you become more adventurous and even start to enjoy it. As parents continue to give their kids a taste of foods they initially dislike or disguise the bitterness with sugar, milk, or something else, most kids gradually acquire a taste for whatever they're continually fed. When everyone around you drinks coffee and alcohol, chances are you'll learn to do so too, even when the taste is not the most pleasurable at first.

There is also an evolutionary aspect to our tastes. Bitter plants, herbs, and spices offer health benefits that our mouths initially reject but our bodies need. Alcohol, coffee, tea, and yerba mate offer a buzz and an energizing effect on our psyches to the point of making us addicted to them. Zhang-Schmidt says many of these foods that may not initially taste good give us the nutrients we need, and therefore, in the course of our evolutionary history, we've come to like them, and at some point, they taste good to us. Our species would not have survived and procreated if we had not eaten enough calories to power our bodies.

But why do we eat things like chili peppers that result in a burning sensation? It's not that any of us are insensitive to the burning. Psychologist Paul Rozin contends that they give us a pleasurable sensation similar to the feeling we get from other behaviors that are risky but safe. The chili sends a warning signal to our sensory system, but it is harmless. Similar to riding a roller coaster or jumping from a sauna into a cold bath, biting into a chili provides a constrained risk.[3] The more curious you are, the more likely you might go after the thrill of biting into something that makes your mouth feel like it's on fire, all the while knowing you really aren't in danger.

In China, people eat food as much for the texture as the taste. Jellyfish or sliced pig ear don't have much taste but have a texture many Chinese enjoy. The tapioca pearls in bubble tea don't have much flavor, but the boba is fun to chew. Texture too is an acquired taste. Many travelers tell me that "slimy" things are the hardest for them to get down.

The curious traveler experiments with new foods and seeks to understand the origins of what, why, and how people eat. Sometimes it's obvious. You find more seafood in places along the coast, but other times the foods and spices are a rich tapestry of climate, region, agriculture, and centuries of tradition.

Food Habits

The customs associated with eating are just as diverse as the foods you encounter as you travel. The etiquette surrounding what, how, and when to eat is one of the most challenging things to pick up when you enter a new culture. I've been the guest of honor at elaborate meals in Southeast Asia where I had no idea what I was eating or the assumptions about who should eat first, whether I should serve myself or wait to be served, or whether I should eat with my hands or go for seconds. In the moment, I just go for it and hope for the best.

You don't have to go far away from home to experience the wonder of different eating customs. In his best-selling memoir *Hillbilly Elegy*, J. D. Vance from rural Ohio talks about the culture shock he experienced when prospective law firms were wining and dining him and his fellow students at Yale. Soon after he entered a private dining room for a dinner hosted by a law firm, a server asked J. D. if he'd like some wine. He said, "I'll take white," assuming he had dodged his first bullet of breaking into a class that wasn't really his own. But when the server went on to ask, "Would you like sauvignon blanc or chardonnay?" he went with chardonnay because it was easier to pronounce.[4]

After sitting down, the server asked J. D. if he'd like tap or sparkling water. J. D. writes,

I rolled my eyes at that one: As impressed as I was with the restaurant, calling the water "sparkling" was just too pretentious—like "sparkling" crystal or a "sparkling" diamond. But I ordered the sparkling water anyway … I took one sip and literally spit it out. It was the grossest thing I'd ever tasted. I remember once getting a Diet Coke at a Subway without realizing that the fountain machine didn't have enough Diet Coke syrup. That's exactly what this fancy place's "sparkling" water tasted like.

"Something's wrong with the water" J.D. protested. The waitress apologized and offered to bring him another Pellegrino. Suddenly he realized that this fancy water was supposed to be carbonated and taste that way.[5]

Eating customs are usually unspoken and taken for granted, yet deviating from them is one of the first things to trigger you being judged as rude or boorish. One time our family attempted a Madrid pub crawl. This involves moving from pub to pub throughout an evening and ordering different tapas and drinks at each place. We had a blast but were often lost about what to order; how to order; and the protocols about when to pay, how much to tip, and how long to stay at each pub. At each pub, my daughter Emily kept asking for bread and cheese and kept being told no. Finally, she tried again at the last pub of the evening, and the wait staff scoffed, "Of course we have bread and cheese" as if it was the dumbest question they had ever heard. Throughout the evening, it felt like we were being scolded by the pub staff and laughed at by the locals. I had a similar experience the first time I sat down to eat at a British pub and didn't realize I was supposed to order my food at the bar. I finally clued in when I saw everyone else doing it.

Figuring these things out as you travel is part of the adventure. But there are a few things to consider as you explore eating customs from one place to another.

When to Eat?

Cultures have unspoken rules about the appropriate times to eat breakfast, lunch, and dinner. I once attended a conference in Europe that was organized by an American group. Dinner was scheduled for 6 PM with a general session to follow at 8:00. The Europeans were amused and slightly horrified about the thought of walking into a restaurant at 6 PM to eat dinner. A couple of the British guys in our group said, "It's time for a late afternoon tea or a drink but surely not dinner," to which a Spanish woman replied, "Why don't we just eat after the 8 PM session is over? We usually eat around 10 PM."

Eat whenever you like. Just remember that "normal" eating times vary and you may not even find a restaurant open at 6 PM in Buenos Aires or at 10 PM in Chicago. If you eat when the locals do, you're far more likely to get an up-close look at the culture and social life.

The amount of time devoted to a meal is another variation to be aware of. I've run programs in Scandinavia where 15-20 minutes is allotted for lunch and in Portugal where it takes over two hours, complete with multiple courses and wine. Many Western-oriented cultures take a functional view of eating. You eat because you have to, particularly during the day, whereas for many other cultures around the world, eating is a chance to savor the food and conversation.

Why Eat?

A traditional French breakfast is bread, butter, jam, and maybe something hot to drink. Food in France is primarily about pleasure. In Italy, food is about love first and nutrition second. An Italian child's first bite may easily be ice cream. Traditions surrounding eating and meals are in transition all over the world. But even among young generations who may be changing this up, there's still a shared, unspoken cultural narrative about the meaning and purpose of food.

Eating is a communal event in most cultures around the world. During the Islamic season of Ramadan, many Arab families and friends have a daily meal called the iftar that breaks the day of fasting together. They eat from the same dishes with their hands, the meal often lasting a couple hours or more. Extended families often eat iftar together every day, but mosques, schools, markets, and other community organizations also offer large iftar meals open to the public daily. Hospitality is a longtime tradition among Arabs. When an Arab hosts a guest, they are expected to put out a wide variety of food and insist their guests eat some of everything.

In contrast, a Qatari friend told me that he and his wife were visiting the United States and a business associate invited them over for lunch. Soon after arriving, they sat down and had a lovely cheese and broccoli soup with bread. They sat there for the longest time as the Qatari couple wondered when the main course would be served. After about an hour or more of conversation, the American couple brought out a plate of cookies. The Qatari couple was shocked when they realized the soup was the whole meal. They weren't offended; they were just struck by how different this was from how most Arabs would approach hospitality.

My daughter Grace becomes unnerved when we go to an Asian restaurant in the United States and she observes people each ordering their own dish. "What are they doing? Who wants to only eat pad thai for dinner? Why don't they all share the dishes they order?" She has experienced the delights of communal eating with shared dishes. Across the world, eating is social, even in cultures where people order their own unique meals. Having a taste of each other's food, sharing your favorite meals on social media, and even waiting in line to get in a trendy restaurant are all part of the social aspect of eating. Anthropologist Richard Wilk suggests that the origins of eating for all of us are social. Enjoying a shared dish of hummus or a fresh pot of tom yum soup or waiting two hours in line to go to a trendy restaurant is all part of the social context of eating.

Hands, Chopsticks, or Silverware?

Italians often say that the quickest way to spot a foreigner is when someone twirls their pasta on a spoon. Italian children learn to put their fork into a few strands of spaghetti, rest the tines against the curve of the plate, and twirl the fork around until they have a serving that can be lifted to their mouth. Unless you're eating soup, spoons are for amateurs and people with bad manners. Worse yet is cutting your pasta with a knife and fork. Long noodles are meant to stay long. It's said that the character of a person can be determined by how they eat pasta.

If you want to blend in with the local culture, using the utensils used by locals is key. Most European diners hold the fork in the left hand with the tines down while continuously holding the fork and knife while eating. But the North American style is to switch the fork back and forth to the right hand, and forks are typically used with the tines up. When you aren't using your left hand, you're taught to place it in your lap rather than leaning on the table. American hand switching is said to stem from a lack of forks among the pioneers, which resulted in the use of spoons in their place. With most people being right-handed, thus holding the spoon steadier with that hand, the practice of changing hands after cutting became socially acceptable table behavior.

Meanwhile, chopsticks are the norm in China, Japan, Korea, and Vietnam. Confucius believed that knives and forks represented aggression and violence and should never be found at the table where you sit with friends and family. And so it's said that chopsticks were designed to not only move food from your table to your mouth but to also reflect gentleness and benevolence. See what your curiosity can teach you from something as simple as eating utensils?

There are some interesting superstitions and customs associated with chopsticks, including these:

- If you find an uneven pair at your table in many Confucian cultures, it means you're going to miss a boat, plane, or train.
- Dropping chopsticks is believed to bring bad luck.
- Diners will sometimes cross their chopsticks at a dim sum restaurant to show the waiter that they're finished and ready to pay the bill. Or sometimes the waiter will cross them to show that the bill has been settled.
- Leaving chopsticks so that they stick out of your food is a major faux pas, as it's done only at funerals when rice is put on the altar. And passing food from your chopsticks to someone else's is also frowned on.
- Usually, the oldest or highest-ranked person picks up the chopsticks first, and the rest follow. If you are the highest-ranking person, they will invite you to begin eating.

Across Africa, South Asia, and much of the Middle East, eating with your hands is normal. Just avoid using the left hand as it's traditionally considered inappropriate. One Indian friend told me, "Eating food with a fork and spoon is like making love through an interpreter!"

It's up to you whether you adapt to the eating preferences of the culture you visit. But you can learn a lot about a culture through the use of their eating utensils or the lack thereof. Use the customs associated with eating as a fun, experiential way to learn about a place.

Paying the Bill

What about the sometimes awkward, unspoken rules about who pays the bill? In the UK, each person at the bar buys everyone a round. In the US, the person who invites the other person out to eat is expected to cover the bill unless explicitly stating otherwise. But there's still an expectation that both parties should offer to pay lest you seem presumptuous. If the person who invited you pays, it's quid pro quo next time. The assumption is you return the favor.

In many Asian and Arab cultures, paying equals prestige. If your host invites you out to dinner, the best way to show respect is to say thank you and not put up a fight for the check. This is true in many Latin European cultures as well. Many of these hosts will discretely make arrangements to pay the bill privately.

In the United States and Canada, once you've been offered dessert and coffee, the server will bring you the bill. But in most cultures around the world, you have to ask for it. It's believed that only a rude waiter brings the check without being asked because you may well intend to linger at the table for another hour or two talking and ordering more to eat or drink.

Many travelers have been confounded by figuring out the proper tipping etiquette in whatever place they visit. The norm in places like Australia and Spain is to simply round up the bill slightly unless it's exceptional service. Whereas in places like the US, 15 to 20 percent is pretty much a standard expectation with many restaurants doing the math for you at the bottom of the receipt. When you go to Japan, however, tipping can be seen as insulting. It's impossible to keep all this straight, so even today, if I can't recall the tipping protocols for a place I'm visiting, I simply do an Internet search when I arrive to guide what I do. And I often verify the information I find online with one or two locals.

Respectfully Declining

What do you do if you really can't stomach something your host serves you? Or what if you have legitimate dietary restrictions due to religious or health reasons? You have every right to forego eating or drinking something. But be mindful that for many cultures, food is a significant part of their identity. If I offer you a peanut butter sandwich and you tell me you aren't a fan of peanut butter or you have a nut allergy, I'd prefer you be upfront with me and not suffer through eating it. But I can't assume that's the same approach others want.

For many cultures, food is a direct expression of who they are. Some people in India use spices that come from plants that have been in their homestead for multiple generations. The best Indian meals take days to prepare. To pass on eating dishes prepared for you in that context could be far more insulting than a visitor at your dinner table passing on a dish they just don't care for. It can be seen as an all-out rejection of your host.

Try not to refuse food or drinks too strongly. If you cannot eat or drink something, tell the host ahead of time so they can plan accordingly and not lose face.

What about the excessive drinking that often happens among business associates in Japan, Korea, or China? Unlike most Western business dinners, business itself is usually the least talked about topic during a business dinner in these contexts. If anything, it's saved for a sliver of time at the end of dinner. But don't think this means the dinner is a waste of time. The purpose of the dinner is to solidify relationships. It's a big part of determining whether you're trustworthy. Expect personal questions, and don't be afraid to talk about your personal life. And if you keep drinking, it will be seen as a symbol of friendship.

But beware. Chinese wine is generally about 40 to 60 percent alcohol and is poured into small cups, which resemble miniature wine glasses. Basically, each cup is like taking a shot of hard liquor. The more you drink, the more pleased your cohorts will be, because it shows you're willing to get drunk with them, just like you would with your friends. To drink with a new business associate is to be brought into their inner circle. It's believed that drinking together deepens and strengthens friendships because it loosens people up and helps relieve misunderstanding, no matter how tense the situation might be. Granted, there are times when excessive drinking is used to wear you down. But the primary orientation behind this practice is social yet directly tied to business objectives.

If you decide to drink very little or not at all, just realize that you're going to have to work extra hard to develop the kind of bonding and relationship building that would otherwise come from the drinking rituals. And if the reason you're not drinking is health related, just state that upfront. But work extra hard to enjoy the food you're served. If you turn down the alcohol, eat the snake that's served.

Food Fuels Curiosity

Sit with a group of travelers, and one of the best topics of conversation is comparing notes on food experiences while traveling. Food is one of my absolute favorite parts of traveling. Eating is one of the few things we all do, and it's one of the best ways to build relationships. Yet social contexts are where our cultural differences often become the most pronounced.

Sometimes when I travel, my host assumes I want to eat at a burger joint. I appreciate the sentiment, but I'd much prefer to eat local. Trying the local foods of a place is fun and educational. And food is one of the few forms of entertainment shared across nearly every culture. It's an adventure. I've been served fried maggots, dog, snake, monkey brain, and endless servings of fish head curry. I've eaten the eye of many fish with my dining companions watching my every move. And there are days when I've been traveling for a long stretch and the familiarity of a bagel and Americano at Starbucks is just what I need for breakfast.

Use the exposure to different foods as a way to curiously explore the history and values of a new place. You just might discover some new comfort foods along the way.

Curiosity Challenges | Food

CQ and curiosity allow you to gain more from the culinary adventures that come with travel. Withhold judgment—plan, check, adjust. And use CQ to communicate your eating preferences.

Low CQ and Closed	High CQ and Curious
That's disgusting!	How do you eat it?

- Try something new wherever you go. It will whet your curious appetite, give you a taste of something local, and provide you with a new food to add to your regular diet.
- Look for the meanings behind the foods you eat. Find out whether certain foods are associated with certain holidays or events.
- Identify the ingredients most commonly used in local foods. Why? Can you find this ingredient at home?
- Observe the eating customs (e.g., utensils, time of day, who pays) and see if you can make sense of why those are the customs. Try following the customs for a day or even your whole trip.
- Come up with a way to communicate "no, thank you" if served something that you cannot or would prefer not to eat. Practice it with someone.

5

Dilemma: You Have 84 Kids?

What makes you think someone is rich? Is it the kind of car they drive? Where they live? Their clothes? When is the last time you thought about someone's wealth based on how many kids they have?

My friend Isaac is the oldest of 84 kids. The first time he said that I thought he was joking. He wasn't. His father, a chief of a village in Liberia, has kids from a dozen wives. This isn't uncommon in places like sub-Saharan Africa. Paul Malong, the former chief of staff of the South Sudan Army, has more than 100 wives and hundreds of children.[1] I've often arrived somewhere, and it takes me a few days to figure out which kids belong to which parents and how everyone is related. It gets downright confusing to figure out who is family and who isn't, especially since terms like *uncle* and *auntie* are used in many cultures to simply refer to any senior adult.

In many cultures around the world, the more family you have, the more people respect you. And the younger the woman you marry, the better. A 13-year-old can bear many more children than a 20-year-old can.

Many travelers have the idea that there is one type of family—theirs. For Westerners, *family* usually means a nuclear family with parents and children. But in much of the world, your family of origin is the most important part of family, even as an adult. Family usually includes a strong bond among parents, grandparents, aunts, uncles, and cousins, sometimes all living in the same household.

Few things will stretch your comfort zone more than encountering different families as you travel. Most of us have deeply rooted beliefs and assumptions about family. It's the first social group we encounter in life, and we tend to assume there is only one kind of family—ours. But as we start to experience other families, we begin to see that even within the same culture there are wide variations in how families go about life together. Observing and interacting with families as you travel provides another way to learn more about yourself and the world.

Family Roles

Every married couple has experienced the stark contrasts between one family and another. When my wife and I were dating, it appeared we grew up in pretty similar families—dads who worked multiple jobs so our moms could stay home to raise the kids, church as the center of our social lives, adherence to a conservative Christian belief system, and much more. But after we got married, we discovered some profound differences. Everything from how to cook spaghetti to expectations around the way to spend Christmas Eve was rooted in starkly different traditions and assumptions.

Take money for example. In my family, my dad oversaw the finances. In Linda's family, her mom did. We never talked about this at the time, but when we got married, we both assumed we'd be the one balancing the checkbook and paying the bills. The much bigger issues surfaced when deciding how much financial risk to take, whether to buy another car, or how much to splurge on a vacation.

I was recently talking with a senior vice president of a global bank in India. She told me that she still passes every paycheck to her mother-in-law and has to ask her for the ATM card when she needs some cash. Why does a senior executive with exposure to the modernized world of global banking pass her mother-in-law her paycheck? This is the way it's always been in her family. Many of us choose to change our behaviors compared to how we were raised. But our families strongly shape why we do what we do.

My daughter Emily and I recently spent a couple days in Brunei. We walked through Kampang Ayer, the world's largest water village. It's a collection of more than forty villages with over 39,000 people who live in houses on stilts above the river. This is the kind of thing we love to do when we visit a new place, roaming the streets and seeking to respectfully encounter life up close. From afar, the houses look like ramshackle fishing shacks, but up close you see beautiful homes surrounded by balconies draped with freshly washed sarongs, bedding, and woven mats; orchids and bougainvillea fill whatever empty space remains. Young kids and grandpas pull up fishing nets in between answering calls on their smartphones and lifting weights. The Bruneian water village has medical clinics, mosques, fire and police stations, shops, schools, and markets with a maze of metered water mains and electrical powerlines beneath. Many of the homes have at least three generations living together. Grandparents live under the same roof as their adult children and grandchildren. The oldest male in the family brings his bride to live in the family home. The daughter-in-law is expected to be submissive to her mother-in-law who oversees the entire household. This is consistent with life across much of Asia and many other cultures too. As with many trends, this is beginning to change but not as quickly as you might think.

Across many Asian and Latino cultures, the father functions as the primary authority figure. For matters outside the home, the father most often serves as the decision-maker and spokesperson on behalf of the family. Many Asian fathers would expect to be the one to sign a consent form allowing a medical procedure to be performed on their adult child. This is quite a contrast from the United States where health care professionals are forbidden from discussing adult kids' medical issues with their parents.

Who is your family? How you answer that is in large part a reflection of your cultural background. Traveling and encountering other approaches will inevitably make you reflect on your own family.

How Do You Say "I Love You"?

I only recall one time when I heard my mom say, "I love you." It was the day my dad died, and even then, it was hushed and said quickly in response to me saying it first. My dad never said it to me, and I never heard my parents say it to each other. My parents both grew up in reserved Canadian homes originating from British and Irish roots. I never really thought about "I love you" being said in a family until I married my wife whose family says it every time they talk.

When I first started to think about the absence of "I love you" being spoken in our home, it struck me as a sign of dysfunction. But my time spent with several Chinese families got me thinking about it differently. This is one of the benefits of international travel. It can shed light on things that happen in your own upbringing that you often miss until you're on the other side of the world.

Chinese parents and kids often maintain what others might perceive as a distant relationship from each other. Gabby Leow, a Chinese American university student, interviewed several of her Chinese peers, and they were in agreement. It was rare that they or their parents said "I love you" to each other. Chinese parents have as much affection for their kids as other parents do but rarely state that explicitly.

One of the students said, "I can remember the few times when I have actually heard my parents say, 'I love you.' … It is not a common thing but very memorable when it happens." Instead, parents communicate their love by saying things like "Put on your jacket" or by asking, "Are you sleeping?" and "Have you eaten?"

In fact, many of the university students agreed that when their mom or dad call them, the first thing they ask is, "Have you eaten?" Their parents demonstrate their love and affection through food. One Chinese mother said, "All of my feelings are inside the food… . If I make his favorite food, it's the easiest way for me to express my love. And he can feel it by eating my food… . All my feelings, all my love are in the food I make."[2]

I've learned to rest in the confidence that my parents' way of expressing their love for me hasn't come through speaking the literal words. But their faithful support and investment in my life in countless other ways makes the actual words have little significance. I guess we've broken this norm in my family because my kids and I say "I love you" to each other daily. But my interaction with other cultures has broadened my view and makes me less quick to judge how people express affection.

What Do You Do for Math?

If saying "I love you" varies from one family and culture to the next, how about education? For example, how much did your parents invest in teaching you math? Many Asian parents create a mathematically rich environment from the time their kids are small. They play math games in the car, on the playground, and at the dinner table and talk about numbers, shapes, and patterns all the time. When walking through the supermarket, they say things like, "If one apple costs 80 cents, how much will six apples cost?" It's not uncommon to be on an elevator with an Asian mom who says to her preschooler, "We're on the fifth floor. How many floors will we pass if we take the lift to the eleventh floor?"

When Maya Thiagarajan moved from the United States to Singapore, the question she always got from other Asian mothers was, "What do you do for math?" Maya was a bit taken back by the question. After all, she prided herself on being an involved parent who immersed her young kids in a language-rich environment by reading to them, taking them to museums and concerts, and playing many imaginative games with them. But descriptions of these activities did little to appease the mothers she met in Singapore. The same question would always arise: *What do you do for math?* Full conversations would revolve around this question of how parents should provide their kids with a strong math foundation.

Maya grew up in India but spent most of her adult life in the States until her husband took an expat assignment in Singapore. Early childhood and elementary education in the US are primarily focused on language and social skills. Parents are socialized to see the importance of giving their kids a love for reading and creativity.

Maya reversed the question to other Asian moms she met in Singapore: *When do you read to your kids?* They responded by talking about their kids' daily routines, including going to school, participating in extracurricular activities, and going to tutors. After all that, they would come home, eat dinner, and collapse in bed. But Maya kept asking, "So when do you read to them?" Just as Maya didn't have a direct answer to "What do you do for math," most of the mothers she talked to said reading was something that got covered at school where they teach kids phonics. After all, the parents said, reading is fundamentally rooted in math skills—practice, drilling exercises, and looking at the structure of words and sentence—and Singapore continues to top world rankings on standardized test scores measuring reading, writing, and math. But Maya challenged her friends to consider whether they were teaching their kids critical thinking abilities.[3]

There are a lot of theories about why Asians excel at math and American kids at creativity. But the most compelling research points to one thing—it's the *attention* put on these subjects and skills at home that makes the biggest difference. Since parents require it, the schools emphasize it, and Asian kids end up more readily excelling at math while American kids do well at critical thinking and creative writing.

Look for these emphases as you travel. Nearly every mall in Singapore has a store devoted to selling math workbooks. Most decent-size towns across Europe have a bookstore filled with literature. As we continue to see, curiosity is not *if* you pay attention, it's *where* you direct your attention.

The families you encounter as you travel offer you a mirror from which to see yourself and your family values.

Do You Eat Your Parents?

The first time I heard a Chinese friend say "I'm a parent eater" I knew this had to be a matter of bad translation. I quickly filled in the awkward silence with, "Tell me more." He explained to me that parent eaters are young adults who still rely on their parents for financial support, beyond a socially acceptable age. I responded with, "Oh! Got it. I don't think that's unique to China. That seems to be happening everywhere now," not exactly the response of a culturally intelligent, curious traveler.

It's true that adult children's financial dependence on their parents is a global trend. But the cause in the Western world is mostly due to the financial demands that have come with student debt, low wages, and the mounting costs of living on one's own. About 20 percent of Americans in their twenties and early thirties live with parents, and 60 percent receive financial support. A similar trend exists in the United Kingdom, Germany, Italy, and France.[4]

Young adults' financial dependence on their parents has been a reality in China for much longer and for different reasons. There's a high level of intergenerational dependence in Confucian cultures, particularly among Chinese. The first generation takes care of the second generation; then later in life, the second generation is expected to return the responsibility. In traditional Chinese culture, it would be unusual for someone to move out of their parents' home until they marry. Some of that is changing, but the intergenerational view of finances and ownership continues to be starkly different from the Western world.

US consultant Zac Dychtwald spends a lot of time in China. The most common question he gets asked there is, "Is it true American families cut their child off financially after the age of 18?"[5] Many young adults in China continue to depend on their parents even after they move out, get married, and have decent jobs. Dychtwald says what surprised him most were the thirty-something adults making above-average wages, living on their own, while still relying heavily on their parents' financial support.

The Chinese culture is the most collectivist in the world (see the appendix). There's a highly interdependent view of decision-making, responsibility, and ownership. This collectivist identity results in less emphasis on the financial responsibilities and opportunities for an individual couple. It's more about the financial state of the family at large. A young couple's first home is often a mix of savings from the couple and multiple generations. And this interdependence goes far beyond finances. Chinese young people talk about the phenomenon of "seven aunts and eight uncles," the reality that their extended family believes they have every right—and more than that, the responsibility—to ask about every aspect of their lives—their love life, finances, eating habits, sleep schedule, food shopping, and on and on. One young married guy says that when he goes home, his aunt takes his wife aside and wants to know how often they are having sex and then proceeds to give her advice about how she should be doing it and when.

To what degree do you retain interdependence with your parents as an adult? This varies widely, and it's one of the most challenging issues for couples that intermarry from different cultural backgrounds. One way isn't better than the other. But assumptions about the role of your parents in your married life may quickly illuminate profound cultural differences. As you travel, talk with your tour guides and acquaintances about their relationships with their parents, siblings, aunts, and uncles. Beware of assuming that their experience is normative for everyone else in the culture. But when they say something that surprises you, say, "Tell me more."

13-Year-Old Brides

What about polygamy? Should a curious traveler simply view a guy with 100 wives, some of whom are mere adolescents, as merely a cultural difference? This is one point where Western liberals and conservatives unite. Nearly all agree that polygamy is disgusting and wrong.

Curiously understanding a cultural practice doesn't equal agreement. But am I truly curious if I merely try to figure out why you do what I have already concluded is a vile practice?

What if we could suspend judgment about something like polygamy for a moment and genuinely take a curious, open mind to what's behind the practice?

Polygamy is one of the oldest forms of institutionalized wealth, particularly when it's in the form of polygyny—one man with multiple wives. Across most of history, marriage has not been primarily about love or sex. It's a means of defending your family from your enemies. Among the Yanomamö people in South America, what makes a man prominent is not his fierceness but the number of kinsmen he has.[6] In most tribal societies, a few men have enormous numbers of offspring with many wives. Acquiring females of reproductive age is one of the most prized measures of success.[7] However, most men in polygamous cultures have only one wife, and a few guys even have to share a wife because there aren't enough to go around. A few men remain single—perhaps the "Western" equivalent of being a down-and-out homeless person.

Polygyny creates a high degree of stress and anxiety for young men. When a rich man has a Lamborghini, there are plenty of less expensive cars available that people with less money can drive. But that isn't so with wives. There are only so many women in a village, and every time a rich man marries another wife, there's one fewer woman available for the other men.[8]

The Yanomamö have a social arrangement called the brother/sister exchange. This is how it works. You marry my sister and I'll marry yours. As a result, you will be motivated to look out for me and I'll do the same. The alliances carry across multiple generations. The inevitable outcome is that most Yanomamö men marry a woman who is simultaneously his mother's brother's daughter as well as his father's sister's daughter, something referred to as a bilateral cross-cousin. As a result, your wife's brothers become your allies. You and your brothers gave them your sisters in exchange for their sisters; therefore your political and reproductive interests overlap.

When Westerners criticize polygamy, they rarely stop to consider all this. The first thing most Christian missionaries do when they enter a tribal society is to teach about polygamy as evil. Historically, a converted polygamist was taught to divorce all his wives except the first. But where do the children go? If they stay with their father, they're often mistreated by the one remaining mother. Some progressive missionaries have changed their approach to keeping polygamous families in tact while calling converts to avoid taking on additional wives.

Most agnostics are equally critical of polygamy, mostly because of how it leads to the exploitation of women. And most Western academics who argue for progressive views on cultural relativity about sexuality and morality draw the line when it comes to tolerating polygamy. Allowing a culture to arrive at its own values and norms is suddenly seen as repressive and backward. There's reason for their concern. Many women in polygamous societies are forced into marriage, physically abused, and left without a voice in their future. But it's unfair to characterize that kind of abuse as normative for all polygamous societies.

I'm not for a moment defending polygamy. A growing amount of research points to the instability and violence that stems from polygamy. It leads to all kinds of troubling issues for the individuals and societies involved, which is why most cultures around the world are moving away from it. Even if exploiting women isn't the intent, it's often the inevitable outcome because women become viewed primarily based on the children they produce. But before being too quick to condemn it, we would be wise to curiously consider what's behind it and use that curious investigation to better discover the wonders of how differently we go about family life based on where we're from.

As you travel across the Middle East, sub-Saharan Africa, and many parts of Asia, you'll encounter polygamy. Beware of your assumptions when you ask questions about parents or spouses and strive to suspend judgment.

Love Marriage versus Arranged Marriage

A French executive recently told me that a young Indian woman who works for her is about to get married. It's an arranged marriage. The French executive took the young woman aside and said, "Look. You know you don't have to do this, right? This is the twenty-first century! Women can marry whomever they want. I hope you're not feeling pressured into this from your parents!"

The Indian woman was taken aback and assured her boss everything was okay. The French executive pushed further: "Well, do you love this man?" The young Indian woman replied, "That will come. We have the rest of our lives."

Many Westerners get riled up over the idea of arranged marriage. From a Western perspective, marriage is about finding the person you love and choosing the person with whom you want to build your family and future. The judgment from Westerners on this is strong, even from progressive people who are typically understanding and respectful of cultural differences.

Many individuals from cultures that use arranged marriage are equally judgmental toward love marriage. I was talking to a group of young men in Chandigarh, India, who asked me if my marriage to Linda was arranged by our parents. I gave them an abbreviated story of how we met and fell in love. But I could tell they were skeptical. It seemed inconceivable to them that a marriage put together by two young twenty-somethings would really last. How could we possibly know whether our compatibility would last? As a twenty-something, it would have seemed inconceivable to me to let my parents choose my spouse. As one who has been happily married to Linda for more than 25 years, I'm often amazed myself that we managed to find each other in our twenties, particularly because we've both changed a lot in the years we've been together. Love marriage and arranged marriage are simply different ways of structuring family.

How does an arranged marriage actually work? The process varies widely with forced marriages on one extreme and consensual ones on the other. In a forced marriage, the bride or groom, or sometimes both, have no choice in the matter. The parents or extended family decide that two individuals should be married, and that's the end of the story. In some cases, marriage involves a young girl being physically forced to become a bride, something the United Nations now condemns as a human rights violation. But most arranged marriages look nothing like that. Instead, parents, and most often mothers, seek a good match for their sons. Through a combination of networking, socializing, and creating opportunities for the couple to spend time together, multiple facets are considered: the compatibility of the couple, the ability of the individuals to support and complement one another's families, and a subjective sense about whether this is a good match.

Arranged marriage takes a more practical approach. Careful consideration is given to finding the partner who will be most compatible with the family's interests and goals. Western marriage is much more caught up with romance. There is the quest of finding the person to whom you're attracted, and while compatibility is certainly considered, the chemistry and shared interests between two lovers are more dominant. Westerners can be thought to be leaving their love lives to chance. We won't always stay attractive and youthful, so what happens to the passion when the lust is gone?

A number of studies reveal that arranged marriages last longer than love marriages. Psychologist Robert Epstein spent ten years studying arranged marriages in a variety of cultural groups including Indians, Orthodox Jews, and Pakistanis. He interviewed over one hundred couples to assess their commitment and connection to each other and found that, on average, by ten years into marriage, couples in arranged marriages describe twice the level of love and commitment than those in love marriages do. And the divorce rate among arranged marriages is significantly less.[9]

Hmm … I wonder why that is.

A number of factors should be considered. For example, Western marriages are much easier to get out of. With 50 percent of US marriages ending in divorce, parting ways isn't easy but is considered a viable option. If you feel trapped or lose interest, society encourages you to move on, and individuals are empowered to leave abusive or unfaithful partners. In arranged marriages, the commitment runs deep. It's between families and not just individuals. Divorce is still looked down upon by most of the cultures that use arranged marriage, and every effort is made to keep the marriage together.

The curious traveler needs to recognize the beauty and value of different approaches to marriage. Millions of couples fall in love and choose to get married to spend the rest of their lives together. The same is true of couples in arranged marriages. After more than 25 years of being married to Linda, I'd choose her as my life partner all over again. So while I've argued for a curious, nonjudgmental approach toward arranged marriage, the same is needed for the traveler who views love marriage suspiciously. Both approaches can work. Don't rush to judgment; seek to understand.

All in the Family

Our families shape our view of the world more strongly than any other influence. Sometimes we choose a different approach to life from how we were reared. But our families are forever a reference point. Families can be one of the greatest sources of joy and are equally poised to inflict some of the deepest emotional pain we experience.

If you have a chance to enter someone's family circle as you travel, do it. You learn so many things about a culture by observing the family dynamics. Beware of judging too quickly but use your curiosity to observe and understand. Don't assume your approach to family is best but neither assume that other cultures' family systems are superior.

Curiosity Challenges | Family

Our families are the first people we ever encounter; as a result, we form strong beliefs and values around how families should behave. Curious travelers use their cultural intelligence to expand their view of family relationships.

Low CQ and Closed	High CQ and Curious
No one should have that many kids!	I wonder how that works.

- Talk with locals about their favorite family gatherings. When do they gather? What do they do? How does this compare with your family gatherings?
- If you get invited to a family's home, go! You'll get a whole new insight that you'll never get from hotels and restaurants. Just beware of applying your experience from one family to all families from that culture.
- See if you can meet three locals who will share with you how they got their names. After they introduce themselves, ask them about the origin of their name, who gave it to them, and when a name is given.
- "Tell me more" is a great response when you're confronted with an approach to family that is unfamiliar or jarring to you. See how many times you can use it in a conversation this week.
- Identify the "hard line" for you ethically when it comes to marriage and family relationships. How might your beliefs about this be different if you had been brought up elsewhere?

6

DILEMMA: WHY DOES "YES" MEAN "NO"?

Why would someone give you the wrong directions rather than say, "I don't know"? It's hard enough to wade through different accents and languages, but when you add the confusion of people meaning different things from a word as simple as *yes*, it becomes utterly confusing. I grew up in New York where you say what you mean and mean what you say. But that's not the norm in most places around the world.

Our family was recently in Delhi. One morning we woke up to so much fog and smog that you couldn't even see out the hotel window. We were supposed to be taking a morning flight to Varanasi. I called Air India, and they assured me that the flight was on time. As we checked out of the hotel, I said to the guy at the front desk, "I wonder if our flight will be delayed." He just laughed and said, "Yes, sir," and sent me to the concierge to get a taxi. I said the same thing to the concierge and again to the taxi driver, and they too just laughed and said something like, "Your flight will be okay, sir." What does that mean? It didn't really answer my question.

Our hotel was no more than five minutes from the airport, at least that's how long it took when we arrived. But it took us nearly 30 minutes to get there. Granted, traffic delays are not uncommon in a city like Delhi, but this was mostly because the taxi had to crawl due to the fog. When we finally checked in at the airport, I asked the Air India agent whether the flight was on time. He assured me it was. There would be no delays. I was amazed and a bit skeptical. I soon learned my skepticism was well founded. By the time I got through security, I could see that every flight listed was delayed or canceled. All flights were grounded for the next several hours, but I continued to receive nebulous responses when I asked about our forecasted departure time.

Predicting the weather is impossible, regardless of the culture. But it's the way of communicating about it that can be so frustrating. I experience this kind of thing all the time when I travel. I stop to ask for directions and I'm sent the *wrong* way—as in someone confidently telling me where to go and it's in the direct opposite direction of where I should have gone. If you've ever watched the TV show *The Amazing Race*, you see this all the time as teams frantically ask locals for directions only to find out the people they asked didn't really know what they were talking about.

I would much rather someone say "I don't know" than assure me I'm headed in the right direction. I'd rather be given bad news straight—"The flight is not leaving on time"—than receive empty promises.

Why does this so often happen? Is it just a language barrier? Is there a different value placed on telling the truth? Or is it something else?

As usual, it's rarely that simple. But if you learn to use your curiosity and CQ to lean into these kinds of communication dilemmas, not only do you get better information along the way, you also gain a critical strategy for working and communicating more effectively with people from diverse backgrounds at home. You just might become a more deft, savvy communicator wherever you are.

Yes, No, Maybe

First, let's tackle words as simple as *yes* and *no*. As you travel, *yes* can mean many things. It may mean "I acknowledge you have spoken to me," or "I understand you think the flight may be delayed," but it most certainly may *not* mean, "You are correct."

Yes and *no* are simple words for most Western communicators. You simply say "no" or "no, thank you" and move on. Communication is filled with nuance for all of us. Tone of voice, body language, and other nonverbal behaviors play a part in what gets communicated. But in most Western cultures, *yes* means "I agree with you," "You're correct," or "I will do that." *No* means the opposite.

In most other cultures, it's entirely different. In many Asian cultures, it is considered impolite to say no. Instead, one might say, "That may be difficult." To a Westerner, that means, "Okay. This is a challenge. Let's figure out how to solve it." But from an Asian, *difficult* may mean, "This task is impossible," "I don't want to do this," or "It's difficult, but I will try."

Other versions of saying no are "Let me think about that," or "We will consider this and research it further." If I heard one of those phrases from someone in Asia, my guess would be it means they aren't interested and have no intention to do anything more about it.

The curious traveler won't automatically assume anything. But you're wise to at least beware that "Let me think about that" may not for a moment mean they need more time to think about it. Perhaps the most frustrating form of no for many travelers is silence. You send a message to someone with whom you've been communicating, and they suddenly stop responding. Silence is often a gentle no.

Every individual and culture falls somewhere along a continuum of direct versus indirect (see the appendix). Even Western cultures have variations in how direct they are. If you ask a Dutch person, "Would you like something to drink?" they will more than likely respond directly, such as, "No, thank you." British culture values a less blunt approach so the more typical response might be "I'm okay, thanks." Many Americans respond, "I'm good." By the way, imagine how confused a nonnative English speaker might be if someone says "I'm good" in response to the question, "Would you like something to drink?" What does being good have to do with it? But it reflects a communication style that avoids an overly blunt no.

What if you ask a simple question like, "Is the train station that way?" Often, indirect communicators will tell a stranger "yes" even if they don't know whether it is. It might be because they aren't sure they understood the question and want to avoid losing face by asking you to explain it. Either way, there's likely a desire to not let you down.

Then there are those shopkeepers in stores you enter as you travel who say "Yes?" the minute you enter their store. Nothing else. Not, "Good afternoon, how may I help you?" Just "Yes?" This used to really irritate me. It seemed rude. I hadn't asked them a question so why are they saying yes? On top of that, they would usually follow me around the store. I later learned that the context behind "Yes?" was that this shopkeeper probably assumed I was busy and needed something. The implied meaning behind "Yes?" was *Let me help you find what you're looking for so I can save you time and let you be on your way.* Following me had a similar intent. That reframing changed everything for me. Suddenly I loved the efficiency of the approach.

Indirect communication often gets a bum rap from Westerners who describe it as passive-aggressive, obtuse, or disingenuous. Don't assume an indirect communicator is being dishonest or lacks confidence. The indirect communicator who says, "Let me think about that" is more than likely politely telling you no. You just might have missed the full context of their communication to you. One of the benefits of becoming a curious traveler is you become much more adept at accurately understanding what people are communicating because these differences exist even among people from the same cultural background. Neil Miller, an expat in India, says the person who learns to understand and speak indirectly has developed a true art. You need skill, nuance, and sophistication to use something other than the blunt edge to speak to and understand others. This goes so far beyond yes and no.[1]

Self-Serve versus Butlers Everywhere

Which do you prefer? A sign with explicit instructions as you enter a hotel or a personal greeter who welcomes and guides you through the process? Walk into many hotels across North America and Europe and there are minimal staff visible. Using mobile check-in, I can now fully check in and out of a hotel without having ever talked to someone working there. At luxury hotels in the Western world, there will usually be at least a bellhop and concierge, but even then, you often have to specifically ask them if you want help with your luggage or to get directions. Walk into even a modest hotel in the Middle East or Asia and you will easily be greeted by four to six staff before you even make it to the reception desk. Several of the staff will welcome you, ensure you know where you're going, and insist on helping you with your luggage.

Hmm … I wonder why that is.

A similar contrast occurs at train stations or airports around the world. If I step off the train in Berlin, there are signs everywhere. All I have to do is read the signs to find a taxi, the restroom, tourist information, and a whole lot more. If I step off the train in many other places around the world, no such thing exists. There might be a few signs, but everyone seems to know what they're doing and where they're going. If I look too clueless, someone will inevitably come up to me and ask, "Where would you like to go, sir?" In most cases, my host would have sent someone to meet me right at the platform, although they may not be there by the time I arrive.

I used to insist on handling my own luggage when I arrived at a hotel where people are scrambling to help me. I travel light and can easily handle my roller board bag by myself. But I began to understand that I was shirking the staff's desire to serve. And paying a tip to someone who brings my bags to my room is a small way I can help someone whose monthly income may be less than I'm paying for one night at this hotel. Inevitably, the individual who brings my bags to my room insists on giving me a tour of the room and explaining the various amenities. Do I really need to have them explain how to use the TV remote? Not usually. But there's an underlying value focused on providing personalized instruction and guidance.

This same personalized approach to communication applies to rules. I recently went for an early morning run at a park in central Kuala Lumpur. I had been running there several mornings in a row, but on this particular morning, a guard started yelling at me and telling me I wasn't allowed to run at the park in the morning. "The park is closed. You must leave." I was miffed. *If it's closed, why don't you have a sign telling me it's closed? And if there are certain hours you aren't allowed to be in the park, just post a sign saying so.* But in high-context cultures, being corrected by another person is a typical way of regulating behavior rather than posted signs.[2]

These communication differences carry over into written contracts.

Anytime you rent bikes or surfboards or do some kind of activity with a tourist company in the Western world, there is inevitably a detailed written contract spelling out your responsibilities and liability. When our family rented motor scooters in Myanmar for a day, the rental agency, which was a couple of women sitting alongside the road in plastic chairs, didn't even take our name or a deposit much less ask us to complete a written agreement. In much of the world, your word and your handshake mean far more than a legal document created by distant attorneys.

If you travel for work to China, doing business is primarily about developing personal relationships. Going out for drinks or dinner after a meeting is a far more important part of developing a business partnership than agreeing to written terms. This stems from the popular Chinese notion of *guanxi*, which means "connections" or mutual obligations to one another. If you achieve guanxi with someone, it means you've developed a relationship characterized by trust, mutual obligation, and most importantly, shared experience. Passing up a dinner invitation may cause you to lose the deal. Chinese companies may draw up contracts to please their Western business partners, but one should not be surprised if they want to alter the terms the day after the document is signed.

Haggling over Price

Travelers encounter the curious differences in communication through something as simple as shopping. In direct cultures, prices are rationalized and everyone pays the same amount. In most parts of the world, haggling over price is how business is done. It's rarely as simple as "how much does it cost?" Bargaining is a complex process of give and take. The goal is to avoid offending the seller while working to find an agreeable price with as little information exchanged as possible. If I name my maximum, the seller may be insulted or may find out I'm willing to pay more than they expected. But I have to find out the seller's minimum to determine whether we can reach a mutually agreeable price.

Bargaining usually involves more than just talking. The successful shopper typically uses gestures and facial expressions and may threaten to walk away and buy from someone else. The specifics vary from one culture to another. But as you learn to curiously observe and experiment with haggling, you just might pick up negotiation strategies that may be useful in all kinds of other contexts. Indirect communication requires a different level of nuance and deft than direct communication.

I should interject that I think some travelers go too far in haggling. I've been with groups who pound their chest with pride for having bargained a shopkeeper down from $2 to 50 cents. Granted, $2 may be way beyond what a local would be charged, but do we really want to be the travelers that pride ourselves on never spending a bit more than the lowest amount possible? Yet as most of these things go, it's complicated. If shopkeepers consistently get 400 percent more by selling to a tourist, it will discourage them from doing business with locals. Just stop to consider some of the deeper issues that lie beneath haggling and negotiating as you shop. I'd rather pay a bit more for a souvenir I buy from someone trying to make a living than boast about negotiating a local down to a rock-bottom price.

The skill you learn when haggling at a local market carries over into international business negotiations. The standard approaches taught in many negotiation courses are directly opposed to the conflict-averse nature of many relationship-based cultures.

My wife is a negotiator's nightmare. We bought our house from good friends. I wanted to get the price lower than they were asking so our realtor wrote up an offer. We eventually reached a price agreeable to all of us, but Linda was distressed by the whole thing. When we talked with our friends about it afterward, Linda said, "I'm so sorry you didn't get what you wanted for the house." They just laughed and said, "Business is business! This has nothing to do with our friendship." I agreed with them. But there's no such thing as "business is business" in most places around the world. Life revolves around relationships.

Ironically, many of the negotiations I'm involved in with our international clients involve a far more arduous, bureaucratic process than negotiating with a US company. Confirming a contract with a company in Mexico or Qatar often includes an endless filing of documents, following a litany of procurement protocols and more.

Hmm … I wonder why that is.

I've also noticed that many of the phone conversations I have with international clients go immediately to business, rather than the perfunctory small talk that typically characterizes the first couple minutes of many US business calls. These realities seem like a contradiction to the more relationship-oriented nature of these cultures.

As always, none of these ideas can be over generalized to any individual or organization, but many international companies have put a long list of systems in place to minimize corruption. In addition, similar to having a guard stand at the park to tell people they can't run at certain hours, these organizations have large departments of people monitoring the rules. If everything checks out, a person signs off to approve the contract rather than just putting it through a system. Most US companies minimize bureaucracy because it impedes efficiency. In many other contexts, the bureaucracy reinforces the power of certain individuals who need to be part of signing off on a contract and vendor.

In some ways, negotiating a contract with many of our international clients resembles the kind of relationship-based haggling that happens at a market. The process often involves a lot of personal conversations and text messages with leaders inside these organizations who become dear friends.

The Feedback Sandwich

Sometimes work-related travel involves communicating difficult information to an international counterpart. If something isn't going well, many companies decide it's worth the time and expense to do it in person. Given the nuanced approach to communication we've been discussing in this dilemma, that's a good idea. But how do you communicate criticism cross-culturally? Western managers are taught to use the "feedback sandwich"—start with something positive, bring up the criticism, and then end with something positive and hopeful. I'm not a fan of the feedback sandwich. The positives strike me as disingenuous if they seem to be added merely to lessen the blunt edge of the "real" point of the conversation. But not everyone wants constructive criticism the same way.

Erin Meyer, author of the excellent book *The Culture Map*, describes a meeting she observed where a group of international managers discussed some of the challenges they were facing. Willem, a Dutch manager, said he was confused about how to resolve a conflict with his Asian clients. His colleague Maarten immediately responded by saying, "You are inflexible and can be socially ill at ease!"

Meyer felt extremely uncomfortable as Maarten publicly scolded Willem while the rest of the group sat there listening. Later that evening, the group had dinner together. Willem and Maarten were eating, drinking, and laughing together like old friends. Meyer said, "I'm glad to see you together. I was afraid you might not be speaking to each other after this afternoon."

Willem looked surprised by her comment and said, "It doesn't feel good to hear what I have done poorly. But feedback like that is a gift," he added with an appreciative smile to Maarten.[3]

More direct communicators use "upgraders" to intensify negative feedback using words like *absolutely* or *totally*, such as "That is absolutely unacceptable." Indirect communicators use "downgraders" to soften the blunt edge of criticism, such as *kind of, sort of, maybe,* and *slightly*. When an indirect communicator says, "I don't think we're quite there yet," they more than likely mean, "This is unacceptable."[4]

Any discussion about all these communication differences would be incomplete without a discussion of "face." Face is the social dignity, respect, and prestige an individual and community work to develop and maintain. In Confucian cultures, for example, one never utters a word or takes an action without calculating the effect on face. This is particularly important when dealing with superiors or colleagues, as when verbal disagreements are muted and indirect signals are used in negotiation. Yet it can be equally important to respect the face of subordinates. These are high-power distance cultures (see the appendix) in which the boss is expected to be authoritarian, perhaps bark orders, and deal harshly with employees who disobey. Yet the boss should not embarrass employees in front of others when they make a good-faith effort to do the job right—unless they have bungled so badly as to lose face already. This can damage morale and may even erode the boss's authority in the eyes of other employees. Confucian authority carries with it a paternalistic duty, and careless disregard of face indicates lack of care for one's subordinates. Face is a powerful force and must be used wisely.

Face also carries over into seating arrangements. Where you sit and who sits next to whom is a big deal for planning dinners in high-context cultures (see the appendix). In Korea, car seat arrangements are planned out, with the most senior in the designation in the rear right seat, rear left for the next in line, and most junior in the front next to the driver. Communication goes far beyond words.

Face is an important part of communication among many Latin American cultures too. In Mexico, face is tied to the importance of machismo or masculine honor. A Mexican business conversation can be very different from one north of the border in the United States. The purpose of conversation is as much to build trust between business partners as to exchange information, particularly in the early stages of the relationship. There is a lot of talk about family, because a good family person is someone of honor who can perhaps be trusted in business as well. The relationship is not based so much on mutual obligation, as in the case of guanxi, but at its best, it's based on an emotional bond of friendship. US businesspeople talk business in a business meeting; anything else is an aside.

Mexican business conversation is about the whole person. It is important to keep the emotional radar on to remain sensitive to how the other party is reacting. In particular, one should take care not to embarrass the other by alluding to mistakes or shortcomings, because this brings loss of honor.

What Side of the River Did You Grow up On?

Where do all these differences come from? Why does a gate agent from Lufthansa say, "Your flight will surely be delayed" while one from Air India says, "It should be okay"? One reason may be the abundance of wheat grown in Germany and rice in India. Wait, what? Yes! What a region grows and the effort required to grow it is believed to play a role in the kind of communication style that exists.

Thomas Talhelm from the University of Chicago conducted a fascinating study focused on the different values, behaviors, and thinking that emerged from different sides of the Yangtze River in China.[5] As Talhelm traveled throughout China, he noticed people in northern cities like Beijing were much more forthright and direct while people in southern cities like Guangzhou were more reticent and deferential. He decided to explore this further and examined the differences across 28 provinces in China. He suspected that wealth or modernization might be the strongest contributing factor, but it wasn't. Instead, the most consistent correlation between the thinking and communication differences encountered was whether they came from a region that grew rice or wheat. Regions to the north of the Yangtze grew wheat while those to the south grew rice.

Growing rice requires a high degree of cooperation. People need to stay in the same geographical region and play their part in tending to the crops and building irrigation systems. Growing rice requires elaborate systems for sharing water as it moves from one patch to the next. University of Michigan researcher Richard Nisbett says that relationships within one's community provide both the chief constraint in people's social lives and a primary source of opportunity. Generation after generation of people in farming communities must consider all kinds of social relationships when making important decisions. When confronted with a conflict of views, they naturally orient toward avoiding the conflict or resolving the contradictions neutrally, known as the middle way.[6]

In contrast, wheat farming is a much more independent quest. The biggest variable is one's hard work and the annual rainfall rather than intricate irrigation systems and large work crews. Wheat farmers do not need to collaborate with their neighbors nearly to the degree that rice farmers do; therefore, they can focus on tending their own crops.

Talhelm worked with colleagues in China to survey more than 1,000 students in various rice and wheat growing regions. The researchers used a measure to assess Individualism versus Collectivism (see the appendix) where people are asked to draw a diagram demonstrating their relationships with their friends and associates. People from individualist communities usually draw themselves bigger than their friends and family whereas people from collectivist cultures usually make everyone the same size. The Chinese students who grew up in wheat-growing regions drew diagrams that looked more individualistic while those who grew up in rice-growing regions drew ones that looked more collectivist. Talhelm even found this to be true in border communities along the river where on one side wheat was grown and on the other side rice. The pattern continued.

Talhelm later tested his hypothesis in India where similar results occurred between wheat-growing and rice-growing regions. Nearly all the Chinese and Indian youth surveyed were not directly involved in farming. However, the cultural heritage from their families had been socialized. The curious traveler stops to consider why people do what they do, including themselves. It's less important to know for sure why you speak as directly or indirectly as you do. Simply the value of stepping back to consider the origins of how you communicate gives you a better appreciation for diversity.

What's Behind the Yes or No?

I often talk to travelers who tell me they aren't always sure whether the locals they meet overseas understand them. Inevitably, someone chimes in with, "Just ask them." But that rarely works, particularly if you're communicating with someone who uses a more indirect communication style. As I travel, even when someone tells me something confidently, I've learned to keep checking with multiple sources and to find alternative ways of getting the information instead of just asking outright. And I stop to consider how my communication may be confusing to others.

Curiosity Challenges | Communication

You're not going to change the patterns of communication that have existed in a culture for many centuries, nor should you try. Instead, the curious traveler is on a quest to find ways to deal with people as they are, rather than how you think they should be.

Low CQ and Closed	High CQ and Curious
They lied to me!	What did they mean by that?

- Practice using some of the different communication styles you observe with your fellow travelers to see if you can broaden your own communication repertoire (e.g., more or less blunt, eye contact, distance you stand from each other).

- If you're traveling with others, take turns navigating to the next activity. See who can get there on the first try. Require that everyone stop at least one local to confirm the directions.

- Use haggling to practice direct and indirect communication. Make it a competition with your traveling companions. Who can get the best price without upsetting the store owner?

- Don't assume you understand. Find creative ways to clarify such as paraphrasing what someone has said or purposely saying back the opposite of what they've told you to see if they correct you.

- Ask locals what they observe about the communication styles of people from your culture. Would they know your nationality just from talking with you? Why or why not?

7

DILEMMA: WHAT DO YOU MEAN BY "NOW"?

A manager in South Africa said that no matter how hard he tries, he can't get his staff to be punctual. He's tried every motivational strategy he can think of, but it still makes little difference. A black South African leader challenged him. "So how do *you* get to work in the morning?" The Afrikaans manager appeared perplexed by the irrelevance of the question but responded by telling him what route he takes. He acknowledged there are times when the robots (traffic lights) aren't working or he runs into a traffic jam, but he builds in time for those unexpected delays and so should others.

The black South African leader said, "Well, imagine you're getting to work every day in a minibus taxi. You make every effort to be on time, but there are so many things beyond your control—what time the taxi comes by, how many other passengers will be dropped off. It's nearly impossible to accurately predict the timing. And after several attempts to be on time, you realize it's a pointless effort so you simply do your best and get there when you get there. Life is too short to get all worked up about things you can't control."

Is this a plausible explanation or just an excuse? Surely minibus taxis can't explain the rampant tardiness at many South African companies. Some of the staff who are consistently late drive themselves. Plus, the same people who arrive late to work come late to meetings during the day.

Well, what if you walk by a good friend who shares that her mother is not well? To just pass by that friend in order to be on time to a meeting would go against your very core values.

For many Westerners, myself included, time is a prized commodity. Missing a deadline or consistently showing up late is a profound sign of disrespect. But in most places around the world, schedules and start times seem arbitrary; any number of circumstances or priorities may supersede those. How can the curious traveler approach different perspectives and behaviors around time?

When Are You Late?

JR West, one of Japan's commuter train lines, issued a public apology for leaving the station 25 seconds early. The train was scheduled to depart Notogawa at 7:12 AM, but a conductor's signal was inadvertently misinterpreted, which caused the train to leave the station at 7:11:35. This meant some passengers missed it and had to wait six minutes for the next train. The apology issued by the company read as follows: "The great inconvenience we placed upon our customers was truly inexcusable. We will be thoroughly evaluating our conduct and striving to keep such an incident from occurring again."[1]

Japan, South Korea, Norway, and Germany are places where being on time is part of how you communicate respect. In Germany, for example, the general rule of thumb is to arrive five to ten minutes before the start time. But most of the world treats schedules and start times much more flexibly. In Mexico, Brazil, or Saudi Arabia, you're unlikely to be considered late until 30 to 45 minutes after the start time. In Malaysia, if you let people know you may be a few minutes late, you have at least another hour before most people would think twice. In Morocco, it's said you can be anywhere from an hour to a day late for a personal meeting without people giving it much thought.[2]

These are crass generalizations. Don't ever assume it's okay to be late just because you're meeting with someone from a different culture. And this varies widely between one individual and organization to the next. There's also a big difference between personal appointments and work-related ones. But most of the world treats time and schedules flexibly.

On a recent family trip, we landed in Ethiopia late at night. We had a connecting flight early the next morning so I booked a nearby hotel with shuttle service to make the most of the few hours of sleep. The hotel promised there would be a shuttle driver holding our name as soon as we arrived at the airport, but as happens so many times in our travels, that never happened. I eventually found someone from a different hotel who said they would call our hotel, who in turn said the driver was coming "now." Another twenty minutes passed, and I called the hotel directly to see what was going on. Again, they told me he's coming "now," but it was still another thirty minutes before we saw him. Once we finally got to the hotel, another lengthy waiting process ensued to complete the check-in process.

Why do some cultures and individuals prize time as a treasured commodity and others view it much more ambivalently? Why does *now* mean different things in different places? The importance of punctuality, schedules, and deadlines emerged in the Industrial Revolution when there was suddenly a need to organize large-scale factory production. This ensured that workers showed up on time, production moved forward, and customers could expect timely delivery. Time became a commodity; therefore, a great deal of effort was put on tightened schedules and getting a job done quickly and efficiently. Given that the industrial age was birthed in predominantly Protestant cultures, there was dynamic synergy between the cultural moorings of western Europe and this increased commodification of time. Western Christianity has a long history of emphasizing personal accountability, stewarding time to create greater advancement, and a relentless commitment to working harder and smarter to make the world a better place. In contrast, the Hindu belief in determinism or the Islamic focus on inshallah ("if Allah wills") results in a very different orientation toward time. Time is not characterized as an economic resource but is something received in abundance that continues from one day and generation to the next. Islamic culture emphasizes the virtue of patience and regards haste as undesirable. Though all three faiths share a view of life being beyond one's control, Muslims in particular have a much more devout view that God orchestrates every step. A similar predeterminism is found among many Christians outside the Western world.

Meanwhile, much of our modern lives depend on coordinating schedules far in advance. I'm often mesmerized when I think of all the schedules and timelines involved for something as simple as attending a conference in London—arranging things at home for while you're away, booking accommodations, scheduling flights, registering for the conference, and on the list goes. And the same is true for hundreds of others attending the same conference, not to mention the organizers who book the venue, speakers, and exhibitors. It's mind-boggling to think about all the individuals and schedules involved for a couple hundred people to convene for a conference, most of whom have never talked with each other beforehand.

I spent a summer in college volunteering in the Amazon rainforest. Each time we arrived at a new village, we held a town hall meeting where we met everyone. There was no scheduled time for the meeting. I just played my trumpet in the village square and people showed up. For the Pirahã tribe in the Amazon, the only thing that exists is the present moment. There is no sense of the past or the future. As soon as something stops happening, it is forgotten. A missionary tried to teach the Pirahã to count, but they had no words for numbers and not even a cognitive category for it, so the task was impossible. As a result, the quantification of time was simply nowhere within their psyches.[3]

Time is a hidden language that reflects the social contracts we create with each other. It is a major force shaping our lives, and that's one of the reasons it creates so much dissonance when we travel to places that treat time differently. The Pirahã tribe is an extreme example of time difference. Nearly all contemporary cultures quantify time at least loosely. And some of the most popular travel destinations require a lot of advance planning. You may miss out on the chance to visit the White House, the Vatican, or the anime museum in Tokyo if you don't book ahead of time. But the curious traveler holds advanced bookings loosely. A rigid concern for schedules, deadlines, and punctuality is simply not something valued by most people living globally, particularly in their personal lives. And there's little you can do to change that.

Would You Be a Good Samaritan if It Made You Late?

A group of students at Princeton Seminary were assigned to give a speech on the Good Samaritan, a parable from the Bible about a traveler who takes compassion on the destitute. The students were told it was time for them to give their presentations and that they needed to do so in a building across campus. One group of students was told they were late and needed to get to the auditorium across campus as quickly as possible. Another group was told they could head over now but that they had plenty of time before the presentations began.

On the way to the building across campus, each student came across someone who was slumped over, coughing, and in obvious need of help. The students didn't realize this was part of an experiment to see how they handled the choice of helping a stranger in distress versus being on time to give a presentation about being a Good Samaritan.

The majority of students who believed they had plenty of time stopped to help. However, 90 percent of the seminary students who thought they were late didn't stop. They went ahead and gave their speeches about helping people in distress and later acknowledged that they saw the individual but knew their time constraints left them with no option to help.

The subtle manipulation of time caused virtuous, well-intentioned seminarians to put punctuality and their immediate concerns ahead of the welfare of someone clearly in need of help. The way you treat time is ultimately a reflection of what you value. We all value time. We all value money. We all value relationships. But it's how all these values work together that differs starkly among us as individuals and cultures.

Time is the most popular word in the English language.[4] We expend a lot of energy on how to get more time, and one of the alleged perks of money is that it gives you more time. You can pay someone to clean your house, avoid public transit, and buy gadgets to make you more efficient. Yet people in wealthier societies seem to have less time than people in poorer ones.

Perhaps you've heard the African proverb that says, "You have the watches. We have the time."

My daughter is dating a South African. When she asks Anthony how soon he'll be ready to leave, she's learned that "just now" means something different to him than her. For Emily, "just now" means he's ready to walk out the door. To Anthony, it's an unknown amount of time. It could be a few minutes, or, as explained in one article about South African time, "just now" may refer to minutes, tomorrow, or never.[5]

For many cultures around the world, an event begins when it begins. It's not about some arbitrary time created before anyone knew what kind of weather, circumstances, and unexpected events might be going on that day. And so in these kinds of cultures there's a flexible understanding that life's circumstances can't possibly be anticipated with any consistent accuracy so why expect timeliness of yourself or others?[6] This goes directly against an individualist (see the appendix) who has a strong internal locus of control, believing that most circumstances can be managed and time is what you make it. Schedules and deadlines can almost always be met because except in rare circumstances, the individual can control the outcome.

Deadlines and schedules are held loosely in most cultures around the world. There's more priority on timeliness in most work settings, but as soon as you get outside work, most cultures have a much more relaxed treatment of time. One of the most important steps for dealing with frustrations surrounding time begins with understanding the vastly different perspectives and values cultures have surrounding time.

When Should I Expect You?

Imagine that your tour guide Jake shows up 30 minutes after the time he agrees to meet you. Jake expects you will do the same. Is Jake late? If this is Jake's consistent practice, you must simply remember to tell Jake to come 30 minutes earlier than you plan to meet him. This is the way dinner engagements usually work in France. If you're invited to dinner at 7 PM, you're expected to arrive around 7:30.

But if you and Jake agree to meet at 7 PM, and you show up 30 minutes before he does, now you're inconvenienced. You could have spent that extra time doing something besides waiting for Jake. Frustration ensues when the equilibrium is off between two parties' expectations about time.

The first time we were living in Singapore, I didn't have Internet access at home so I had to travel to a local Internet café. Internet shops were abundant in Singapore, but I specifically wanted a place that would let me connect my laptop to the Internet so I could download my e-mail and read it offline. That in itself was a daunting request for many of the cafés I visited, but I eventually found one willing to accommodate me. Their hours were 10 AM to 7 PM, but I soon learned there was no consistency to whether they would be open by 10 AM. For that matter, sometimes I showed up in the middle of the day and the place was closed, with no sign explaining why. And this was in Singapore, a very Westernized, contemporary society. Many shops I visit around the world don't even list their hours.

Can you change the way you or others treat time? If Jake the tour guide has always treated time flexibly, can he change that orientation to suit travelers like you (or vice versa)? Surely anyone can be more punctual or flexible when needed, but can you change your core orientation toward time?

For the most part, we retain throughout our lives the cultural values socialized in us as kids. If you're brought up with an individualist identity, you will likely go through your adult life thinking and living as an individualist more than a collectivist. The same is true for your orientation toward time. Growing up in my family, my parents typically built in extra margin when heading to an event to allow for unexpected delays. I've instilled that same value in my kids. But unlike personality, our cultural identity is not hardwired into us. Culture is not an innate, predetermined trait. It's dynamic and evolves as we exercise our agency and choice, which over time can begin to change a culture as a whole. But cultural values don't change quickly.

Economists Basu and Weibell have done some fascinating research that suggests our time orientation has little to do with our innate preferences. Instead, it's a choice we make based on our perceptions of others' expectations. If others are on time and expect me to be on time, it's more likely I will be punctual. It might take a while, but most Italians moving to Germany will eventually adjust their orientation if they continue to experience disgust from colleagues annoyed by their tardiness. But if others are notoriously late, the time-conscious person (e.g., me) will probably start arriving late as well because they gain no benefit from being early if no one else shows up then. You're unlikely to change your core time orientation during a brief sojourn in a new place. But after repeated encounters that reinforce an expectation of punctuality or tardiness, most people align their behavior to match the expectations of others living and working where they are.[7] It's about finding an equilibrium between both parties.

If you live overseas for a while, one of the hardest parts of returning home is adjusting your time orientation. I have many friends who have moved to cultures with a more flexible orientation to time; when they return to the United States, they're disoriented by everyone's obsession with a regimented schedule. I have other friends who have experienced the direct opposite. Moving to a time-conscious place like Switzerland and heading back to the reverse in a place like India can cause enormous frustration.

Our orientation toward time becomes deeply ingrained, and we experience dissonance when we suddenly have to alter it. Showing up on time or meeting a deadline requires effort. As one who highly values that, I would argue that the extra effort alleviates all kinds of stress and frustration in the long run. But that's because I consistently interact with others who are expected to be punctual. The effort I devote to being punctual is only valuable if others do it.

Past, Present, or Future

When you're traveling, do you think most about what your experiencing in the moment, memories from previous travels, or the future? My head is forever in the future. What's next? Where will I be in five years? What should our next destination be? This drives my wife crazy. Linda is one of the most present people I know. If you send her a text message, you're unlikely to get an immediate response from her because she's 100 percent focused on what's going on in the moment.

Whether you focus on the past, present, or future is a phenomenon studied by world-renowned researchers Phillip Zimbardo and John Boyd and is something they refer to as your *time perspective*. According to Zimbardo and Boyd, our behavior and state of mind are strongly affected by the way we think about the past, present, and future. As psychologist Mihaly Csikszentmihalyi says, "How we feel about ourselves ... ultimately depends on how the mind filters and interprets everyday experiences".[8] Our minds powerfully shape our lives, and our perspective on time has a big influence on how we travel and see the world.

Time perspective refers to your emotional attitude toward time. It's your mind's way of parsing life into the past, present, and future. Most of us rarely stop to think about the powerful effect of time on our lives. Yet our time perspective is associated with so much of our emotional health and behavior. We develop our attitudes toward time through personal experience and upbringing, but collectively, our attitudes toward time are shaped by our cultural surroundings.

Confucian cultures like those found in China, Korea, and Japan place a great deal of value on the past. This may seem inconsistent with the soaring skyscrapers and modern technology you experience when you visit these places. It's an interesting paradox. Confucian cultures are oriented toward the past as a window into the future. There's a long backward orientation to provide guidance on how to look several generations forward.

This is one of the things I love about travel. When you encounter vastly different views of something as central as time, it triggers reflections on your own sense of time. Your perspective on time becomes a silent governor of how you live your life and communicate.

What's your time perspective? When you think about the past, is it mostly positive? Do you look back on previous events with a sense of gratitude and nostalgia? Or is your view of the past more filled with a sense of regret and pain? In part, this is influenced by the stability of your childhood and social support available to you. People who grew up with a low level of support from family and friends are more likely to view the past negatively. Yet there are people with traumatic upbringings who still manage to look back on the past with a sense of gratitude for the person it forced them to become. And there are people with storybook childhoods who view their positive upbringing with a sense of regret.[9]

A series of studies comparing Germans and Americans' sense of time illuminates the role of culture in an individual's time perspective. Germans are more likely to look at the negative implications of past events while Americans are more likely to focus on the positive. German poet Goethe wrote, "Let me pass the nights in tears, As long as I want to cry," whereas America writer Longfellow wrote, "Be still, sad heart! … Behind the clouds is the sun still shining." American cyclist Lance Armstrong described cancer as the best thing that ever happened to him. German actor Michael Lesch described his cancer as a horrifying experience that created a never-ending sense of anxiety. Culture plays a big part in how we view the past, present, and future. Watch for this as you travel.

Our cultural environments also play a critical role in our view of the present. Feeling discouraged, sad, anxious, or upset is part of life. But our response makes all the difference. Do you spontaneously experience the fullness of the moment and believe life is what you make it? Or is your view more oriented toward a fatalistic sense that things happen beyond your control and you simply have to make the most of it?

How much do you think about the future? Does discussing the future energize you, or does it suck the life out of you? Do you think about the future in terms of your goals and bucket list, or are you more oriented toward spiritual transformation and life after death?

Criss-Cross Time

When we change our clocks in the US to accommodate Daylight Savings Time, I go around the house and change every clock the day before the time changes. I can't stand to have the clocks wrong. And much to my wife's chagrin, I prefer to set the clocks one to two minutes ahead of the actual time, simply to create some margin for punctuality on top of the fact that I already head somewhere with enough time to allow for unexpected delays. My orientation toward time is deeply ingrained, but even for me, if I'm meeting friends or colleagues who are notoriously late, I find myself shifting my expectations because there are few things I like less than "wasting" my time.

As much as I hate to admit it, few things become irreversible because of a missed deadline. Those of you who are time-conscious like me need to take a deep breath and consider this in the whole scope of life. For those procrastinators gloating in my acknowledgment—beware. I've silently decided not to work with some individuals or organizations when I know that follow-through is vital and I just can't risk it—or deal with the added stress. Don't underestimate what your treatment of time communicates.

You're unlikely to change someone's time orientation, much less an entire culture's. Seek to understand why others view time the way they do and work on seeing the value of a different approach toward time.

Curiosity Challenges | Time

Different expectations about schedules, punctuality, and deadlines is one of the biggest frustrations experienced from travel. The curious traveler makes a conscious effort to adjust to the time orientation of the places they visit, at least while they are there.

Low CQ and Closed	High CQ and Curious
She's on Latin time!	How do people know when to arrive?

- Before you travel, take the survey at thetimeparadox.com along with your travel companions. As you travel, notice how your time perspectives influence how you and your fellow sojourners interpret what you observe.

- Talk to people you meet about their time preferences. Reflect on whether you see patterns across certain professions, age groups, or other subgroups within the cultures you visit.

- Use the inevitable irritations you feel with time differences to trigger self-reflection. Why are you so annoyed? What can you learn from this frustration about yourself and others?

- When you visit a culture with a different time orientation from yours, try it. Expand your comfort zone and show up when you think a local would show up. You don't need to change your preferences, but you'll gain more flexibility.

- List three benefits that come from a time orientation different than yours. Don't try to change the time orientations of others. There are merits to punctuality and merits to flexibility. The same applies to a focus on the past, present, or future.

Part III
Travel Guide for the Curious Traveler

The curious traveler knows that memorizing facts about different cultures doesn't fit the complex twenty-first-century world. It's impossible to keep up with all the dos and don'ts, and most of the stereotypes about the people you encounter as you travel don't apply.

Instead, you'll get the most from your travel when you approach it with a curious mindset that allows you to make sense of the situations you encounter on the fly. In this final part of the book, you'll find some key practices for applying the type of curious, culturally intelligent mindset I've been describing so far.

8

PRACTICES OF THE CURIOUS TRAVELER

A few years ago, our family vacationed in Bastimentos, a sleepy island in Panama only accessible by boat. Soon after we arrived, we headed into Old Bank, a little town with a mini supermarket, a few cafés, a couple churches, a police station, and no cars. I felt completely alive. This was a curious traveler's dream! Most everyone we walked by appeared to be locals. And given that there were no cars or roads, it was pretty tough to walk around without seeing the culture up close. While trying not to stare, it was impossible not to get a glimpse right inside people's homes where men were chasing chickens, women were bathing their children, and teenagers were heading off to school up the hill.

All of this was just a short flight away from the US! I felt completely alive.

But then I started to wonder if we were intruding. The pathways around the island went right alongside people's homes. Our home in Michigan sits alongside 11 acres (4.5 hectares) of public woods, and I was trying to imagine how I would feel if I looked out my window and saw a Panamanian family strolling by our house with smartphones in hand.

Travel is filled with opportunities to practice your curiosity. But what's the fine line between a curious traveler and a voyeur? Having explored several dilemmas that face the curious traveler, I want to suggest a few practices to guide how we practice our curiosity as we travel. Practices mean just that. It takes practice to direct your curiosity with cultural intelligence.

Notice, Don't Judge

If you travel with our family, you're forbidden from describing what you see as "weird" or "wrong." Different? Definitely! Weird? According to whom? The first practice for being a curious traveler is to open your eyes and see what's going on without rushing to judgment.

One of the most transformative realizations for me over the past few years has been seeing how significantly my life is shaped by where and how I direct my attention. Given the amount of time I spend thinking, talking, and writing about diversity, the minute I walk into a room, I scan for diversity. Others may walk in and notice something entirely different. My wife is a professional musician, which means her attention is primed to hear musical technique, precision, and interpretation. I listen to her perform and hear a flawless performance. She hears every mistake and wonders how I could have possibly missed the notes she fumbled. These are fairly benign examples of how the focus of our attention shapes our reality, but my point is that our experience and view of the world is largely a product of where we direct our attention. Outputs mirror inputs.

Look back over the past five years of your life. More than likely, your life has been shaped significantly by where you directed your attention. If you had paid attention to other things, your reality and life would be different. In contrast, the things you don't pay attention to don't exist—at least for you.[1]

Curiosity is not *if* we pay attention but *how*. The curious traveler recognizes and pays attention to the novelty of a new situation or place.[2] And the key is to pay attention without rushing to evaluate whether what you observe is good, bad, or different. Your CQ helps regulate your curiosity. For starters, simply notice.

As we travel, we're bombarded by stimuli competing for our attention. Our impulse is to pay more attention to negative things than positive. A concept known as negative bias theory explains that we pay more attention to our fear, frustration, and disappointment as we travel than to joy, happiness, and contentment. Negative emotions are far more powerful than agreeable ones. When you're jet-lagged or stressed about catching the last train of the day or when someone criticizes you, your mind puts more attention on those negative thoughts than the positive ones.

The curious traveler slows down the impulse to evaluate and judge and seeks first to understand. Focus on discovery. And by the way, this same spirit of nonjudgmental observation needs to be applied to ourselves. We often reserve our harshest judgment for ourselves. As you travel, observe what's going on in yourself and others and don't judge. As noted repeatedly throughout this book, evaluation may be needed eventually, but most of us go there far too soon.

Turn your attention away from life back home and focus on the conversations, people, and sights around you. Limit your phone use. If you're multitasking, your brain can't put its attention on what's around you. See things for how they are, not how you think they should be. This small shift in how we observe can help us appreciate and even learn from observations we might otherwise view as weird or even wrong.[3]

Our attention is one of the best gifts we can give ourselves and others. We determine what's important by what we pay attention to and what we ignore.[4]

Look for What's Novel

One of the reasons travel is ripe for catching our attention is it's typically filled with novel tastes, sights, and sounds. I've had the opportunity to travel to more than half the countries in the world, yet I'm still amazed how often I experience places, customs, and cultures that are entirely new to me. Even in the past two years, I've heard myself say multiple times, "I've never seen anything like this."

Novelty and curiosity are best friends. When we experience something for the first time, there's a surge of dopamine in our brain.[5] As we've seen previously, *information gaps* and *uncertainty* are the two primary catalysts for curiosity. Travel is filled with both. We enjoy some measure of threat and puzzle in our lives. This is why we like to play games, watch a scary movie, or read a suspenseful novel. But too much uncertainty results in anxiety competing with curiosity. Our brains love to fill in missing information, and we're wired to minimize uncertainty. International travel is the ideal context for both. It is consistently listed as being among the top three most transformative experiences in the lives of adults. As we experience the jarring nature of being removed from our familiar surroundings, our cognition is disrupted. We often return home learning even more about ourselves and our own country than the people and places we visited, which is immensely valuable too.[6]

Beware. You can travel far away from home and experience very little of the novelty there. It kills me when people go to another part of the world and miss out on the novelty. Vacationers who spend all their time at an all-inclusive resort, study abroad students who stick to familiar foods and peers, or business travelers who hunker down at their familiar hotel chain can be twelve time zones away and experience little novelty. There's a place for these familiar settings and experiences, but beware of what you're missing. Even when staying at a resort designed to cater to people like you, with a little effort, you can leave the property for a while, walk the streets, haggle at the market, take public transit, and have a few meals where locals frequent. This allows you to gain the benefits of both relaxation and curiosity. Or simply try engaging the hotel staff in conversation and learn what you can about life for them.

When you travel, stop and look around you. If you were dropped here without knowing where you were, would you be able to guess your location? This is something I often do when I'm in a new place. I sometimes think, *If what I see around me right now is all I had to go on, I wouldn't even know I wasn't back home.* But then I study it more carefully and start to see things that would immediately offer cues that I'm somewhere different. In other places I visit nearly everything surrounding me is new and different.

Identify three novel things about any experience. Write them down or talk about them with someone. This is something we've done with our kids as we've traveled since they were very little. When we were standing in line at Starbucks in Singapore, I'd ask them, "What's different about this as compared to when we stand in line at Starbucks in Chicago?" "They put jellies in their coffee here," Emily said. Grace observed the woman walking outside on a perfectly sunny day with her umbrella open above her.

Amid all the novelty of a new place, our tendency is to look for what's familiar. We reduce the novelty by noting the similarities to things at home. One of the things I often catch myself doing is comparing it to other places I've been. That's okay. It's part of how our brains scan a situation and make sense of it. But beware. If we overemphasize the similarities, we miss out on what novel situations offer our curiosity.[7]

Exposure to what's novel invariably sparks creativity, hope, and purpose. It can also evoke a sense of danger. But embrace the novelty and use it to discover insights about yourself and others.

Travel, at least when we choose to do it, is voluntary exposure to curiosity. We're intentionally putting ourselves in novel situations that will make us feel curious. Follow your curiosity and use the novelty of a place to discover insights into yourself and others.

Embrace Boredom

Before a trip, it feels like it will be nonstop adventure. In reality, travel inevitably involves a lot of downtime, sitting on a train from one place to the next, waiting in line, or lying awake at night because of jet lag. While novel situations induce curiosity, boredom also does it. Sensory deprivation is a critical catalyst for curiosity.

One of the reasons we so often come up with our best ideas while doing mundane tasks like taking a shower or washing the dishes is because moments of boredom free up our minds to think creatively. Our minds don't like to be bored. We crave distraction. Research has shown that those deprived of light and sound for extended periods crave any kind of input. Curiosity intensifies when it goes unsatisfied. As a curious traveler, boredom is your friend.[8]

Yet who has time to be bored these days? As I travel, rarely, if ever, do I see people who are bored. Smartphones protect us from the monotony of doing nothing. You can fast-forward through boring commercials while watching your favorite show, pass the time waiting in line by scrolling through your social media feed, or sit through a religious service or class by surfing the web and texting. I've even seen security personnel and traffic cops using their phones to alleviate boredom. I recently stayed at a hotel in Kuala Lumpur where security officers were posted in every corner due to a VIP visiting the hotel. Yet several of the officers were leaning against the wall scrolling through their phones every time I walked by them.

Our smartphones are an insurance policy against ever being bored, yet boredom is directly linked to creativity and innovation. Researchers Sandi Mann and Rebekah Cadman conducted a study in which participants were asked to come up with creative ideas for how to use a pair of plastic cups. Prior to the brainstorming session, one group of participants was asked to copy numbers from a phone book while a control group was not given the boring task. The group who slogged through the phone book assignment came up with more creative ways to use the plastic cups than the group spared the boring assignment.[9] The researchers interpreted this as the brain having been primed for something more intellectually stimulating.

What our brains want is new input—fresh, stimulating, and social. First, boredom is the ideal environment for reflection. Waiting in line or sitting at a train station is the perfect time to take stock of our thoughts, feelings, and experiences. Instead of reaching for your phone to scroll through social media, stop and consider what you've been learning about yourself and the people around you. Take stock, process it with another traveler, adjust, and confront your own biases. Keep doing this when you get home. This is one of the richest times to tap the power of reflection—when your travel is still fresh in your mind and you've been ushered back into the world of life at home.

Second, boredom increases our capacity for empathy and perspective-taking. Perspective-taking means stepping outside ourselves to imagine the emotions, perceptions, and motivations of another individual. It goes beyond the platonic admonitions of cultural sensitivity programs that teach "respect for everyone." Instead, perspective-taking steps into the shoes of others and realizes they may not want to be treated the same way I do.

Sitting on a bus in a new place and watching the people around me offers me all kinds of insights I miss when my head is buried in my phone.

Boredom improves the desire for connection. It can even motivate people toward higher degrees of empathy and compassion.[10] It's worth thinking about including a tech cleanse as part of your travels. Try going without picture taking for a day and engage more fully in the moment with your surroundings. Even if you end up sitting with "nothing to do" for an hour while you wait to meet your less than punctual tour guide, you'll have fueled your curiosity muscle.

Interrupt Cognitive Bias

First impressions matter even more than you think. Within seconds, our brains size people up as funny, eccentric, smart, or trustworthy. When we land in a new place, our brains are on high alert for seeing what this place is like and whether we've made the right choice to come here. Travel is fraught with first impressions, and early information about an individual or situation disproportionately shapes our perception of them, something called the primacy effect. If we aren't careful, our first impressions when we arrive may rob us of a fuller, more accurate understanding. Consequently, it's critical we learn how to interrupt our cognitive bias, our brain's default system for quickly sizing up a situation and arriving at a conclusion.

Interrupting bias links back to the importance of observing without judgment. It requires using curiosity to fight against snap judgments about new people and places. Snap judgments aren't all bad. In some situations, they're more sound than carefully deliberated decisions because they stem from years of taking in information and arriving at conclusions. There are occasions where cognitive bias will save you—maybe even literally where you sense danger and need to immediately respond.

Most of the time, however, our cognitive biases get in the way when we travel. They lead us to stereotype people or arrive at faulty conclusions. Our snap judgments stem from our internal mental scheme, something deeply rooted in how we've been socialized.

Malcolm Gladwell describes the power of implicit bias when Coke decided it needed to come up with a new recipe to replace the classic soft drink it sold for years. In blind taste tests, people consistently preferred Pepsi over Coke. It didn't matter if the tests were run by Pepsi, Coke, or a third party. As a result, Coke introduced "New Coke," which tasted very similar to Pepsi.

But New Coke was a disaster. People hated it and wanted classic Coke back. In the real world, no one drinks Coke without knowing it's Coke. We transfer our idea of Coca-Cola to the implicit associations we have of the brand, the image, the can, and the iconic red logo.[11] Worse yet was when Coca-Cola experimented with making Coke clear. The experience of drinking Coke is far more than just the tastes that occur in our mouth. Our minds actually change what we taste and how we experience the drink.

When we make split-second decisions—which we're forced to do as we travel—we're most susceptible to our implicit biases. With the help of cultural intelligence, we can train our brains to think differently and avoid acting on the bias. This comes with extensive practice and experience.

There are many forms of cognitive bias, most of which influence how we travel. For example, affinity bias is the gravitation toward people like us. When we travel, we're likely to view positively people who seem like they're a lot like ourselves. Recency bias is when something that has recently come to your attention suddenly seems to appear with improbable frequency, as in you buy a silver Honda and you start to notice silver Hondas everywhere. Your first few hours in a place can strongly shape your impression. But the bias I've seen influence travel the most is confirmation bias, which is the tendency to interpret events in light of your existing beliefs and assumptions. Once our brain gets a sense of what an individual or culture is like, it naturally looks for information that confirms that initial idea and ignores everything else.

Earlier I described the way confirmation bias affected the charitable volunteers I studied. Many of these groups travel as part of faith-based mission projects. Millions of groups participate in these kinds of experiences every year, and the consistency across what they say about their experiences suggests the influence of confirmation bias. For example, the most frequent comment that emerged from my conversations with North American short-term missionaries was, "Even though these people here have so little, *they're so happy!*" I heard it over and over again. Almost without fail, regardless of the country visited, the group with which they traveled, or the focus of their service project, they talked about how happy the poor locals were.

There is something endearing about hearing a group of middle-class North Americans talk about their amazement that people with so few material resources could be so happy. The challenge is, are the people they encounter really happy? I asked these short-term missionaries, "What made you think they're happy?" To which most responded, "You could just tell. They were always smiling and laughing."

The volunteers went in with a preconceived notion that people living seemingly simpler lives are happier than those who have more money. And when they encountered the locals' smiling faces, it confirmed that assumption.

Are people living with few material goods really happier? Research doesn't support that claim. But most of the volunteers spoke little of the local language so if they were visiting a remote village in a place like Ecuador, the interaction went something like this:

"Hola!" (giggle, giggle)

"Hi!" (giggle, giggle)

"How are you?" (nervous laughter)

"Bien, gracias." (more nervous laughter)

Have you been there? I sure have. The smiles might reflect genuine happiness, but they just as well might be a nervous response that indicates little about one's level of contentment. Furthermore, there are cultures like a small community in New Zealand where extremely polite, smiling reactions are a way of expressing disgust. And in Thailand, there are at least twenty different smiles to communicate at least that many different thoughts and feelings.[12] It's unlikely the locals encountered by most charitable volunteers are any more happy than the rest of us. But these groups go in having heard this again and again so the minute they see a behavior that confirms their assumption, they fill in the blank and repeat it as fact.

We gain more benefits from travel when we interrupt our biases. Start by identifying your preconceived notions about a person or place and then talk with your fellow travelers about slowing down from too quickly making interpretations about what you see.

Intentional Curiosity

Channel your curiosity intentionally. It's one of the best ways to interrupt bias and allows you to leverage the power of curiosity when you travel.

One of the most important research findings on motivation is that most of us pursue a goal with either a *promote* or *prevent* orientation. Think of a goal you have. Maybe it's something like increasing your GPA or running a 10K race. What's your motivation for achieving the goal? Is it more because of what you will gain by reaching it (promote goal), or is it to avoid something from happening (prevent goal)?[13]

A promote-goal orientation toward getting a 3.5 GPA is hoping for a better job or increased chances of getting into the grad school of choice. A promote goal for running a 10K is to enjoy the sense of accomplishment from being healthy and fit. A prevent-goal orientation for getting a 3.5 GPA is to avoid negative outcomes like failing a class or not earning enough money after graduation. A prevent goal for running a 10K is to avoid being overweight or suffering from heart disease.

Either kind of orientation can work. But researchers Park, Van Dyne, and Ilgen find it works best when the strategies used to reach a goal are aligned with the kind of orientation you have. If you're working toward a 3.5 GPA, a promote-oriented strategy may include things like scoring well in quizzes and actively participating in class. A student with a prevent orientation might pursue the same goal by avoiding multitasking in class or showing up late.[14]

What does all this have to do with travel? Your curiosity while traveling can be used to promote things you want to accomplish. That can include discovering a new place, becoming more effective working with others, or being a better problem-solver. It can also be used to prevent unpleasant things from happening, like putting yourself in danger, saying something offensive, or missing out on an innovative opportunity. If your goal is to avoid being pickpocketed while traveling, you can channel your curiosity to strategize ways to increase your situational awareness (prevent goal). If your goal is to gain more enjoyment from a long walk from the hotel to the metro station, it would be best to map out a route to allow you to see and experience things that will pique your curiosity and expand the enjoyment (promote goal).[15] You can also use your curious travel to promote new ways to cook, expand the way you do your job, or work on speaking a different language.

Taking a goal-oriented approach to curious travel links to important research on flow, willpower, and grit. Mihaly Csikszentmihalyi's work on flow is an incredibly important contribution from psychological research that can improve our daily lives. He discovered that people find genuine satisfaction during a state of consciousness called flow. In this state we are completely absorbed in an activity. During a state of flow, we feel strong, alert, and almost an effortless approach to our work. And Csikszentmihalyi found that our best moments in life are not the passive, dormant ones. Our optimal moments usually occur when our body or mind is voluntarily stretched to accomplish something difficult and worthwhile. Travel will offer you far more enjoyment and satisfaction when you discipline yourself to curiously pay attention to your surroundings.[16]

Your curiosity together with perseverance and flow can be a critical part of your success, both during your travels and, more importantly, across the rest of your life. IQ and innate talent certainly play a role in your success. But not as much as you might think. Angela Duckworth, a researcher who has conducted extensive studies on the impact of grit across a variety of populations, concludes that grit counts twice as much as talent.[17]

Tension and frustration are almost always part of curiosity. Therefore, intentionally triggering our intrigue and then persevering to sustain our interest are vital for leveraging the benefits of curious travel.[18]

Keep Your Curiosity in Check

Finally, we need to prevent our curiosity from going too far. And this brings me back to the question from the beginning of the chapter. What's the fine line between being a curious traveler and being a voyeur? Often when I'm traveling, I'll zero in on a passerby and consider, *What is their life like? What kind of job do they have? Where did they wake up this morning? Are they happy? Do they have kids?* But what do I do with those questions?

The Panamanian island our family visited has only recently been discovered by travelers like us. We had lunch one day at a local café and were the only foreigners there. We started talking with the grandmother who runs it. She's lived in Bastimentos her entire life, and we asked her how she felt about people like us coming to her village. What's she supposed to say, right? But in between her hospitable welcome, we picked up on her growing concern that gringos were taking over the island. She was grateful for the new opportunities for business, though she said most of the foreigners stay and eat at other foreigners' businesses rather than trying the local places. She wonders what her homeland will look like in the years ahead. And she sometimes feels like she's simply an object in a museum, being photographed as people walk by her café, which is really just the front porch of her home.

Taken too far, curiosity can cross the line and become an end in itself. Social psychologists Christopher Hsee and Ruan Bowen did a series of experiments to test the "Pandora's box" effect of curiosity. Through four simple and controlled experiments, they demonstrated that curiosity can seduce people to open a box when adverse consequences are expected, even if there is no apparent benefit other than satisfying their curiosity. People are more likely to do something if the outcome is uncertain and potentially risky as compared to when they know the outcome for sure.

One of the experiments used ten pens to test the Pandora's box phenomenon. In the first scenario, five of the pens had a red sticker and five had a green sticker. The participants were told that the pens with red stickers would deliver a painful, albeit harmless, electric shock if clicked but the green ones would not deliver any shock. In a second scenario, all ten pens had yellow stickers. Some of the pens would deliver a shock if clicked and others would do nothing, but the participants wouldn't know which pens were which. Participants clicked more of the pens with the yellow stickers than the green or red ones. Curiosity led them to the risk of getting shocked.[19]

When interacting with people as you travel, it's sometimes better to exercise delayed curiosity. It's not appropriate to walk up and ask an African American, "What do you think about Black Lives Matter?" Neither should you ask a Pakistani if their marriage was arranged or how much someone spent on their home, all questions I've heard travelers ask a first-time acquaintance.

The more you get a taste of curious travel, the more you will want to fill in the blanks. However, without properly getting to know the other person first, these questions can come across as intrusive. This doesn't mean you have to become someone's best friend before asking more personal questions, it just means that there needs to be a certain level of trust and respect established in the relationship. Don't lose track of the questions you want to ask, just *delay* the act of asking. Another strategy is to qualify your question by acknowledging that it may be a sensitive topic. Try *Do you mind if I ask …* or *No need to answer if it makes you feel uncomfortable.* Reassuring someone that you are truly interested in them as an individual rather than as a case study for their culture is key to managing curiosity and fostering effective cross-cultural communication.

Or try depersonalizing it by asking them how people in this context typically feel about something. For example, instead of asking a gay Muslim friend how their parents reacted to them being gay, you could ask, "What's the typical response of parents here when they find out a child is gay?" Then the individual can decide whether to share their personal experience.

Another question that works well is "What's something you wished more people realized about your culture?"

Retain your curiosity but keep it in check. This is why curiosity needs CQ. Like an anthropologist, we need to be careful not to use people to benefit ourselves. Consider how your travels can be mutually beneficial to the people you encounter. Use your curiosity to pursue connections while resolving to do no harm.

Travel, the Ideal Curiosity Lab

If you speak Italian as a second language, the ideal way to practice it is to spend time in Italy and use it. Not only will you get to practice this beautiful language, you'll improve your Italian. The same is true of curiosity. Travel is the ideal context in which to put your curiosity to work. And travel is one of the best ways to improve effectively using your innate curiosity.

While international travel is ideally suited to exercise your curiosity, you can also put it to work in places closer to home. Linger at restaurants, stores, and parks in a nearby neighborhood you don't often visit. We're often blind to the novelty that exists right around the corner. And make the same commitment to suspend judgment and delay your curiosity in those places, where it's sometimes even more difficult not to immediately evaluate a different approach as wrong or weird.

9

Tips for the Curious Traveler

International travel used to be reserved for rare jet-setter types or as a once-in-a-lifetime experience. Today, it's not uncommon for families to go abroad for spring break or for Millennials to pull out their passports multiple times a year. I'm well aware that there are still billions of people for whom international travel, particularly for leisure, is simply not an option. But as the bourgeoning middle class grows around the world, many more of us are traveling.

So much of what I've shared throughout this book is focused on applying a curious mindset to your travel—using your CQ to see what others miss. But what does this look like practically? If you're new to international travel, the Internet is your friend. You can find most any information you need about transportation, mobile phone use, electrical outlets, currency conversion, and more on various travel sites. But here are a few specific tips for traveling with curiosity and cultural intelligence.

Pre-Trip Planning

Becoming a curious traveler begins long before you leave home. Choosing where to go; deciding who to bring; and even the basics of visas, shots, and accommodations set the stage for your curious adventure.

How to Travel on a Budget

When our kids were young, we decided to forego trips to Disney World and Legoland and for less money were able to explore places like China, Guatemala, and even France. People often think you need a lot of money to take your family overseas, but there are ways to do it that don't break the bank. Travel during times you might not typically choose and use your curiosity to discover deals to visit unexpected places. Curiously explore how to exploit the surge of budget airlines and mileage programs that have made getting other places much more accessible. Don't think twice about pulling your kids out of school for a week or two to do it. If you're a university student, forego the hourly summer job and spend a couple months overseas. There are many options available where you can work a few hours a day in exchange for lodging and food.

Look for deals from a major airline hub and go from there or even piece together some flights. You might be able to find a relatively inexpensive flight to Tokyo and then fly a budget regional carrier from there. Plenty of blogs and websites are devoted to helping you find good travel deals. Spend some time researching them or make it a family project to put together a trip that stays within your budget. Try Croatia instead of Paris and Nicaragua instead of Costa Rica.

Bring Your Kids ... or Friends!

If you have kids, bring them! There's nothing like seeing a new place through your kids' instinctively curious eyes. And travel is one of the best educations you can give them when you do it right. Our kids missed some "big" school assignments and events due to some of our overseas travels, and I guarantee you, none of us regrets it for a second. Sometimes this requires some advocacy with teachers. Once, my daughter Emily was stressed about completing her math worksheets when we were in China. She had a good grasp of the concepts, but her teacher required her to complete all the worksheets, even though they were mostly doing the same thing over and over. I intervened. "You could be roaming the streets of Kunming right now and instead you're filling out a worksheet. Enough! Let's go. I'll deal with your teacher." From then on, I was proactive with teachers and let them know I wanted my kids to get the most from the educational opportunities where we were. We expected our girls to be responsible for what they missed but were confident their curiosity and lifelong learning would increase from taking in the culture in the moment. Most of the teachers were supportive and slightly envious. I've discovered so much about curious travel by seeing the world through my kids' eyes.

If you choose a friend to join you, choose carefully. Not all friends are cut out for the kind of curious travel we've been exploring throughout this book. The people you are with will strongly shape how you experience a place. Choose someone who is up for going beyond the must-see attractions to take in the everyday sights most travelers miss.

Accommodations

Where should curious travelers stay? Location, location, location. This saying doesn't only apply to buying real estate. It's become the number one thing I pay attention to when booking travel accommodations. Where is this hotel or private rental located? I'm not really talking about convenience and safety, though obviously those are factors to consider. But I actually mean the kind of neighborhood you're in. Does it provide the right environment to curiously explore the place, or are you hanging out with all the tourists or staying too far away from the action?

We started paying more attention to location after renting a small private residence in Kyoto. The pictures of the place were charming, and when we arrived, they lived up to it. It was a very traditional Japanese home with all kinds of character. But it was located in a major industrial area, a long way from the shops, cafés, and temples that permeate Kyoto streets.

Find a place where you can walk the streets, linger in a local café, and wander through the local supermarket. Avoid the hotel chains you frequent at home. I'm a platinum member with one of the big US hotel chains, but when I stay there overseas, I see mostly other Americans staying there. Local hotel chains and private rentals get you closer to the local culture.

Visas

One of the biggest differences between a culturally intelligent traveler and a novice is preparation. And this includes knowing what you need when it comes to visas. Be sure to find out whether you need a visa to enter a country. Most countries follow a reciprocal policy when it comes to visas. If your country requires people from their country to have a tourist visa to visit, you will more than likely need a visa to visit. Something as simple as visa requirements gives you an opportunity to start learning before you even leave home. You can easily find visa requirements online. By dealing with this beforehand, you'll remove some unnecessary stress when you arrive and be able to engage with curiosity from the minute you hit the ground.

A growing number of countries offer e-visas, which can be done online and without sending away your passport. Otherwise, I recommend using a third-party visa service. It costs a bit more but may save you hours (or days!) of time, and the visa companies know how to anticipate the issues that typically get visas denied. For some nationalities, even transiting through an airport requires a visa. Do your homework ahead of time. Airlines are fined severely if they board someone without a visa to a place that requires it. If they're in doubt, they won't let you go.

Shots and Health

Curious travelers take responsibility for their health without being paralyzed by paranoia. Check with your health department to see what immunizations and health precautions are recommended. Then do some additional searching online to learn from other travelers. I would never encourage anyone to be careless about their health. Just bear in mind that some travel websites are going to give you the worst-case scenario and offer a long list of immunizations needed. There's a big difference if you're traveling to a cosmopolitan area versus somewhere more remote. Talk to others who have traveled there and check out travel forums.

The same applies to drinking water. I've heard travelers ask people in Germany and Singapore whether the water is safe to drink. "Don't drink the water" is the age-old advice given to people traveling to many places.

Being careful about water is one of the most important things you can do, but before you ask, do a little homework. When in doubt, drink bottled water and make sure the cap is sealed.

Packing

Less is more. If at all possible, pack everything you need in a carry-on. Not only will you avoid the stress of lost or delayed luggage, you'll be free from the burden of schlepping a load from one stop to the next. And packing less may force you into local shops to find basic items. Buy your liquids at a local supermarket. There are economical options for doing laundry in most locations, and as long as you're flexible, you can pick up inexpensive clothing or toiletries along the way. The experience alone will fuel your curiosity.

Packing less is a simple way to create more mental space for curious observation. Checking bags takes more time and limits your flexibility and transportation options. By sticking to a carry-on, you'll know you always have everything you need with you. For me, the peace of mind is worth it. And yes, my wife and adult daughters agree.

Free your mind for more creative thoughts by packing important things in a consistent place. I always know where to look for my passport, cash, phone, and chargers. Particularly when going through security lines and pulling things in and out of your luggage, it's easy to misplace things.

Culture Prep

Despite all the work I do in cultural intelligence, I'm less concerned about a traveler doing a deep study about the cultural norms of a place before they go. It's more of a mindset that is needed. Traveling with a sense of respect and curiosity and a reluctance to judge is far more important for a brief sojourn than learning all the dos and don'ts. But at least take the time to know the basic history of a place. Were they colonized? How did the majority of the people end up there? What is the country's relationship like politically with your country of origin?

I recommend picking up a novel or memoir set in your destination. If it's a decent book, the author will have done some research on the place and often has spent some time there. I gain insights into things I experience in a new place by reading a novel situated there. The same can be true about movies situated where you're going. Beware of assuming a book or movie accurately represents a place. But it's a great way to get you thinking about the cultural realities.

Finally, skim the recent news for what's been in the local headlines. And then consider using some of that information as the basis for conversation with people you meet. Not only does it give you conversational material, it demonstrates you have some awareness of topics trending there. The best way to learn about the culture is when you're there. Curiously take it in and then compare what you observe with research-based insights about the dominant norms of a place.

On-the-Ground Essentials

Most of this book has covered how to direct your curiosity with CQ in the midst of traveling. Refer to the Curiosity Challenges after each chapter in Part II to get ideas for how to approach standing in line, eating, or dealing with communication breakdowns with curiosity and CQ. But here are a few additional guidelines for how to apply a curious, culturally intelligent mindset to the traveling basics.

Money Matters

Getting familiar with money and buying things overseas is another built-in opportunity for curiosity and adventure that comes with international travel. Do your research ahead of time to find out whether paying by credit card will be an option. It's getting easier than ever to pay by credit card in many places, but don't assume that will be the case. Particularly in a lot of the best places to eat and shop, it will be cash only. When you do pay by credit card, you'll often be asked whether you want to pay in the local currency or your currency from home. Always go with the local currency. There's a charge for paying in your home currency and there's absolutely zero benefit for you.

Calculate exchange rates and learn about the nation's economy. If it seems like a great deal, curiously consider whether it's a good deal for the locals. The best option for exchanging money in most places is to find an ATM as soon as you land and withdraw the equivalent of US $100 to $200. You'll get the best exchange rate that way, and even with a small transaction fee charged by your bank, it's still cheaper than exchanging cash. Just be sure you check before you leave home to see if you need to get a travel waiver to be able to use your ATM card overseas. And check ahead of time to be sure there are working ATMs available.

Jet Lag

I've read most every strategy out there regarding jet lag. As much as I travel, I still struggle with it, and it seems to be getting worse the older I get. Fight it as hard as you can during the first few days. Your physical and mental energy will have a direct impact on how much you can leverage your curiosity and CQ.

Here are a few rules of thumb; curiously determine the best solutions for you. This is more of an art than a science.

- Set your watch to the new time zone as soon as you board your international flight. If at all possible, attempt to follow the new sleep and eating patterns even on the trip over.
- Eat half of what they give you on the plane, if that. And go easy on the alcohol. You're already getting dehydrated. But drink all the nonalcoholic beverages you can get out of them.
- Force yourself into the new sleep patterns immediately upon arrival. Don't take any naps if you arrive in the morning or midday.
- After you arrive, walk or run outside and get as much sunshine as possible. Light is key. Again, stay awake when it's light but not too late. When it's dark, sleep. Light is the most important thing that influences your circadian rhythms.
- Drink a lot of coffee or tea before noon. If you already drink caffeinated beverages, caffeine can have a strong effect in regulating your wake-up mode. It's especially effective if you go without caffeine for a few days prior to travel.

- Consider melatonin before bed. Many people find that melatonin, a natural nutritional supplement, helps regulate their sleeping patterns.

Being well rested and adjusting to the time where you are is critical if you're going to practice and use your curiosity. Your body and brain need rest.

Safety

Many people I talk to would love to travel but are worried about safety. It's a fair concern because being outside your culture can make you more susceptible to being scammed or ending up in a sketchy neighborhood.

I rarely go somewhere I feel unsafe. Almost without fail, I start my day with a morning run, wherever I am in the world. And unlike many other people I've traveled with, I leave my valuables in my hotel room. If it's an old-school hotel with a big key, I just leave the key at the front desk when I take off for the day. Most anywhere I travel, I stop and talk to people when needed and use public transit. I wish people weren't so fearful of traveling in unknown places, but I'm also aware that I'm not a good judge of what others will consider safe. My travel to over one hundred countries over the last thirty years gives me a quick sense when something seems off. More importantly, I'm a middle-aged, healthy, straight, white guy. I may be far safer than my daughters are. And in many parts of the world, my gay friends are in more danger than me. The same goes for many of my friends who aren't white.

Take the time to research where you're going, but also keep in mind that some people thrive on telling sensational stories about how unsafe a place is, and many times it just isn't true. There are some excellent resources online for women traveling alone; the same is true for underrepresented groups like the LGBTQ community and people of color.

Taxis and Local Transit

A culturally intelligent, curious traveler understands that the customs and practices for hailing a taxi and riding public transit vary from place to place. Public transport is also one of the best ways to curiously explore a place. So do your homework and travel local.

A basic rule of thumb when getting a taxi in an unfamiliar place is to see whether you're going to be charged by meter. If so, the amount owed will be straightforward. If not, be sure to negotiate the rate before you get in. Rates are regulated in some places, but if not, start by offering half as much as you're quoted *before* you get in or do a little homework ahead of time to find out typical rates. Figure out how important it is for you to get a "fair price" versus just getting to where you want to go. Like any negotiation, you don't have much leverage once you're in the car.

Try other forms of public transit too. When our kids were young, riding buses and trains was an easy activity that would keep them entertained and allow us to experience the culture. There are neighborhoods in Buenos Aires, Shanghai, and Chicago that make you feel like you've never left home. But then you jump on a local bus or the metro and you're ushered into the local culture. One time we got on a local train in Yangon so we could travel a bit outside the city to see the countryside. We were having a hard time communicating with people at the train station so eventually we decided to just pick a commuter train to ride for a while and then got off and came back the other direction. It was about six cents a person and far more entertaining than any amusement park ride I've ever been on. I'm not exaggerating to say we could have walked as fast as this train was going. But sitting there watching the locals get on and off, observing the neighborhoods, and taking in the multisensory experience of this train was one of the highlights of our trip.

Food

Trying new foods is one of the highlights of curious travel. Depending on where you're going, find out whether the street food or roadside stalls prepare their food in ways your stomach can handle. By all means, avoid the food from home or the place where all the tourists go and follow the locals into their favorite haunts. Point to what they're having.

A couple years ago, my daughter Grace and I ended up one evening in a little restaurant in a Beijing neighborhood where virtually no English was spoken, and our Mandarin left much to be desired. It was a little awkward, but we saw some amazing dishes being eaten by the people around us so we just started pointing to what they were eating and the staff giggled and brought out what we requested. I'm still not sure what we ate, but it was amazing. We became quite the scene in this little hole in the wall as dishes kept coming and we kept trying them. The food combined with the social experience of our surroundings is a memory we'll never forget. As the late Anthony Bourdain said, "It's those little human moments that are the ones that stick with you forever."[1]

Upgrade Your Experience

If you're looking for an upgrade to first class or a top-floor suite, there are websites devoted to telling you how you can up your chances through credit card purchases and timing. But I want to leave you with a few guidelines on guaranteed upgrades that will last much longer than your 15 hour flight or three-night stay.

Avoid the Prepackaged Tour

Just as restauranteurs tell you that preplanned holiday buffets are rarely the way to get the best food, the same goes with prepackaged tours. Roam on your own, or if a guide is needed, hire one who can take you where you want to go. Boarding buses with hordes of people means bringing the frenzied experience and people from back home with you instead of stepping into the other world awaiting you. And many of the prepackaged tours hinder the curious exploration we've talked about throughout the book. Walk the streets, linger in local markets, and think twice about whether the "must-see" sights are the best use of your time.

If you go to Paris, be sure to include a few days in the countryside. If you visit the United States, don't only see Los Angeles and New York, take in small-town America. Or if you want to visit Dubai, include a visit to Oman, a 30-minute flight from Dubai and a world away. Muscat, the seaside capital of Oman, has none of the bling or skyscrapers of Dubai. The government there has decided to preserve the traditional Islamic architecture. And you can get a trip out to the desert.

When you travel to places a little adrift from the tourist mainstays, your budget goes further, you see fewer tourists, and the locals are often more ready to see you.

To Photo or Not to Photo?

What about picture taking? The last time I was at the Louvre, everyone was taking selfies with the *Mona Lisa*. But no one was really appreciating the masterpiece itself. This is such a metaphor for what often happens among travelers. Stop and consider whether the photo you're about to take is part of your curious adventure or whether it's more about making your friends on social media jealous. Although I'd be happy if I never had to take another picture while traveling, I know it's a meaningful way for many travelers to chronicle their experiences. My wife and daughters take amazing photos and videos, and I'm really glad we have those to reflect on all we experience on a trip. Just consider whether there might be times for you to forego taking a picture and instead be fully present in the moment.

There are times you definitely need to avoid taking pictures all together. The obvious ones include when you're passing through customs or when you see a police officer or military official. Many metro stations, airports, and shopping centers forbid picture taking as well. If you aren't sure, ask. Sacred sites and monuments are another example of places where taking photos may be disrespectful. There are usually signs posted but not always.

Perhaps the biggest temptation for a curious traveler is to take pictures of locals—particularly if they appear different from how people look back home. For years, we've traveled to places where complete strangers run up and want a picture with my girls. The first time it's funny and perhaps even a bit flattering, but before long it gets obnoxious. Imagine what it's like to be on the receiving end of strangers constantly taking your picture. And if you sense that your picture is being taken so a tourist can exploit your poverty, it's downright degrading. The curious traveler draws on their CQ to use photography in ways that are respectful and humanizing. If you are truly seeking to capture another way of life on camera, have a conversation with your subject, make a connection with them first, and then ask their permission. Or see if you can take a picture together.

Use a Little Charm

I hesitate to share this one because it really depends on the culture and situation, but showing a little kindness and deference when making a request goes a long way. Don't act like you're entitled to an upgrade or an exception to a rule. Put yourself in a place of need. Say something like, "I'm sorry. I know I should have noticed that I scheduled the tour for the wrong day and your website clearly states there's a fee for changing it. But might you be so kind as to make an exception this one time and let me reschedule it without a change fee?" It doesn't always work. But many staff are empowered to make exceptions when needed. And it's usually far more effective than threatening to write a negative review or saying you'll take your business elsewhere.

Take control of your situation so you can leverage the opportunity to travel with curiosity and CQ. Over and over I've watched stressed-out customers berate a staff member and demand better service, only to have the staff member refuse. And the next person in line treats the staff kindly and gets the very exception the previous person was asking for.

Kindness and respect vary across cultures. And there's a fine line because if it feels fake and manipulative, it will backfire. A better approach is to genuinely take the time to see the humanity of the person serving you and interact with them as a fellow human being rather than as just some hired hand there to serve you.

Manage Expectations

Travel is often stressful. One of the best ways to get ahead of the stress is to manage your expectations. Delays are inevitable and often beyond your control. The service you receive at hotels and restaurants is going to look different and the standards of safety and cleanliness may vary from what you're used to. But that's the whole point. You're removing yourself from the familiar to get a sense of the rhythms and smells of a new place. And that requires curiosity and patience.

Find the real moments when you travel. The longer I've traveled, the softer I've gotten. The adventures of staying in a hostel or a thatched-roof hut along the Amazon River don't provide me with near the thrill they used to. I wouldn't trade some of those experiences for anything. But because I travel so much, I also don't feel guilty for staying at a place where I can be a bit more comfortable, even if it isn't a completely authentic experience. Figure out your priorities and then strategize accordingly.

Know When to Speak Up

I've repeatedly cautioned against judging different customs and behaviors as weird or wrong. Just because you prefer queuing a certain way or think that parents should stay out of their kids' marital decisions doesn't mean other people's approach is inferior. But this doesn't mean the culturally intelligent traveler is a spineless observer who never evaluates something as unjust or wrong. This is a difficult balance that takes a high level of cultural intelligence.

I come face to face with weighing my values against those of other cultures all the time. For example, I've raised my daughters to be strong women. It unnerves me when I encounter cultures where women are treated as second-class citizens, and I'm not going to nod with manila tolerance if I see a woman being disrespected. The same can be said about places where being gay is illegal or where animals or the environment are exploited.

We have to weigh carefully when and how to speak up when we see something unjust. Before being quick to voice dissent, we better be sure we understand the core of the issue. I shared my thoughts on this when we explored the issue of polygamy in Chapter 5. Start with curiously seeking to understand. Can you explain the point of view objectively? Once you've done so, if you're still convinced there's an unjust custom or behavior, find ways to appropriately engage in conversation about it. If I'm spending a couple weeks in a country where women are marginalized, I'm not going to bring it up in every conversation. But I am going to look for appropriate times to address it. I may purposely violate cultural norms in my interactions with women, regardless of how others perceive it. Then I will consider ways I can advocate for more systemic change in addressing the issue at hand—whether that's putting pressure on the businesses there to change their policies and practices, supporting charitable causes that address the issue, or finding another vehicle to promote justice. There are no easy answers to how we address unjust systems and behaviors, but curiosity and respect can never become excuses for remaining silent.

See Less, Wander More

The most invigorating part of travel is getting up close and seeing a different way of life. If you're visiting Paris or Madrid, don't put so much pressure on yourself to see every art museum and iconic building. In the frenzied effort to get a selfie in front of the Eiffel Tower, you may miss what could have been a relaxing morning wandering the streets, slipping into a café, and having a croissant and coffee.

Don't try to see every sight in a city, much less a country or region. And linger longer in a few places—roam the streets, eat at the local cafés, and soak it in.

In talking about the frenzied pace many travelers keep, Bourdain said, "The sort of frenzied compression of time needed to take the tour, to see the sights, keeps you in a bubble that prevents you from having magic happen to you. Nothing unexpected or wonderful is likely to happen if you have an itinerary in Paris filled with the Louvre and the Eiffel Tower."[2]

Now Boarding!

If you're a novice to international travel, don't be intimidated by it. Many people tell me they would love to travel but feel nervous about going on their own. Start with a place that won't push you too far out of your comfort zone. There are endless travel blogs and websites where you can gain insights from others who travel there. Save your money, set the dates, and go!

What about issues like mobile phones, converters, or medications? If you're new to international travel, you can find anything you need to know about these practical matters online. Check both official sites and travel forums to get the lay of the land. And remember not to overpack. If you forget something, most places will have their own version of the item and you'll have a built-in cultural experience looking for it.

Before I say goodbye, the last couple pages of the book provide activities you can begin immediately to jump-start your curiosity. Then I'll send you off with some parting words.

THE CURIOSITY CHALLENGE

Everyone is curious. But many people stop using their curiosity. It never goes away, but without practice, it becomes dormant. You can get that kidlike curiosity back. You just need to start using it again. Direct your curiosity with CQ to your surroundings. Try, fail, and try again. You're practicing to be a curious traveler.

Here are a few ways to jump-start your curiosity on your next trip. You can start doing some of these things immediately. I've included the Curiosity Challenges from each chapter in Part II and added others you can use before and after you travel. Take a picture of these with your phone and try doing one a day to get your curiosity muscle in shape.

Before Your Trip

- Visit a grocery store in an unfamiliar neighborhood near home. What differences do you see from your neighborhood? Buy a snack you've never tried.
- Walk around your neighborhood and identify two things that someone not from here may not understand or may be surprised by (e.g., level of security, how trash pickup works, the color of the squirrels).
- Follow two to three social media influencers from the next place you want to travel.
- During a meeting or in class, identify someone you don't know well. Imagine what today would be like if you were them.

During Your Trip

- On your first day somewhere new, identity three differences from what you see at home.
- Observe how the local fashion compares to the styles at home.
- Eat for one full day like a local, including typical eating times.
- Do a tech cleanse. Go a full day without your phone or use of any digital device.
- What color do you see more than any other? What color would it be at home?
- Take a picture of the same street corner at three different times of the day. Do it during the week and again on the weekend. What do you notice?
- What kind of interactions do locals have with people working in restaurants, stores, and banks? Is it all business, or do they chitchat as well?

Curiosity Challenges | Queues

Different approaches to queues is one of the things that annoys travelers most. Curious travelers with CQ work on expanding their comfort zone while waiting in line.

- Waiting in line is never the activity of choice. But turn it into a cultural experience. See what you can learn about the culture and yourself. Discuss it with your fellow travelers.
- When standing in line, notice who expects to be treated differently. Are there any consistencies?
- See if you can make it through a whole day of queuing up without getting annoyed. Have a competition with your travel partners to see who can last the longest without complaining about the queuing system.
- Notice whether there are any differences in how different age groups or genders queue in the places you visit. Do people queue differently for different contexts (public transit vs. supermarket vs. bank)?
- Pretend you're briefing a new visitor on the queueing norms for where you're visiting. Explain the norms without using any negative language.

Curiosity Challenges | Food

CQ and curiosity allow you to gain more from the culinary adventures that come with travel. Withhold judgment—plan, check, adjust. And use CQ to communicate your eating preferences.

- Try something new wherever you go. It will whet your curious appetite, give you a taste of something local, and provide you with a new food to add to your regular diet.
- Look for the meanings behind the foods you eat. Find out whether certain foods are associated with certain holidays or events.
- Identify the ingredients most commonly used in local foods. Why? Can you find this ingredient at home?
- Observe the eating customs (e.g., utensils, time of day, who pays) and see if you can make sense of why those are the customs. Try following the customs for a day or even your whole trip.
- Come up with a way to communicate "no, thank you" if served something that you cannot or would prefer not to eat. Practice it with someone.

Curiosity Challenges | Family

Our families are the first people we ever encounter; as a result, we form strong beliefs and values around how families should behave. Curious travelers use their cultural intelligence to expand their view of family relationships.

- Talk with locals about their favorite family gatherings. When do they gather? What do they do? How does this compare with your family gatherings?
- If you get invited to a family's home, go! You'll get a whole new insight that you'll never get from hotels and restaurants. Just beware of applying your experience from one family to all families from that culture.
- See if you can meet three locals who will share with you how they got their names. After they introduce themselves, ask them about the origin of their name, who gave it to them, and when a name is given.

- "Tell me more" is a great response when you're confronted with an approach to family that is unfamiliar or jarring to you. See how many times you can use it in a conversation this week.
- Identify the "hard line" for you ethically when it comes to marriage and family relationships. How might your beliefs about this be different if you had been brought up elsewhere?

Curiosity Challenges | Communication

You're not going to change the patterns of communication that have existed in a culture for many centuries, nor should you try. Instead, the curious traveler is on a quest to find ways to deal with people as they are, rather than how you think they should be.

- Practice using some of the different communication styles you observe with your fellow travelers to see if you can broaden your own communication repertoire (e.g., more or less blunt, eye contact, distance you stand from each other).
- If you're traveling with others, take turns navigating to the next activity. See who can get there on the first try. Require that everyone stop at least one local to confirm the directions.
- Use haggling to practice direct and indirect communication. Make it a competition with your traveling companions. Who can get the best price without upsetting the store owner?
- Don't assume you understand. Find creative ways to clarify such as paraphrasing what someone has said or purposely saying back the opposite of what they've told you to see if they correct you.
- Ask locals what they observe about the communication styles of people from your culture. Would they know your nationality just from talking with you? Why or why not?

Curiosity Challenges | Time

Different expectations about schedules, punctuality, and deadlines is one of the biggest frustrations experienced from travel. The curious traveler makes a conscious effort to adjust to the time orientation of the places they visit, at least while they are there.

- Before you travel, take the survey at thetimeparadox.com along with your travel companions. As you travel, notice how your time perspectives influence how you and your fellow sojourners interpret what you observe.
- Talk to people you meet about their time preferences. Reflect on whether you see patterns across certain professions, age groups, or other sub-groups within the cultures you visit.
- Use the inevitable irritations you feel with time differences to trigger self-reflection. Why are you so annoyed? What can you learn from this frustration about yourself and others?
- When you visit a culture with a different time orientation from yours, try it. Expand your comfort zone and show up when you think a local would show up. You don't need to change your preferences but you'll gain more flexibility.
- List three benefits that come from a time orientation different than yours. Don't try to change the time orientations of others. There are merits to punctuality and merits to flexibility. The same applies to a focus on the past, present, or future.

After You Get Home

- What are the first things you notice after being back? Write them down or share them with someone.
- Find a way to "fill in the blanks" from something you observed while traveling but didn't understand (e.g., if you saw a lot of French restaurants in the Asian city you were visiting, look up where the French influence came from).
- Visit communities or businesses locally that have origins in the place you visited. What do you notice (e.g., how does an Irish pub at home compare with the ones in Ireland?).

- Walk around your neighborhood again and think about what you would point out to someone visiting from where you just traveled.

Epilogue

Curiosity has taken us to the moon, expanded our mastery of physics, and given us a better understanding of our very brains. And curiosity can take travel from a brief adventure to something that has lasting value.

I love going places where everything is new and everything is a surprise. Fortunately for me, I've had the ideal life for a curiosity seeker. And my family shares my quest for discovering new wonders wherever we go. My daughter Grace has always had a particularly curious mindset ever since she was little. In her college application, she wrote:

> Whether it's having porridge for breakfast in China, staying with a family in Nepal, or roaming through grocery stores in Buenos Aires, Johannesburg, Madrid, or northern Michigan, there's always something that captures my attention. Don't get me wrong. I enjoy visiting the must-see sights in places I go but what I love most is encountering people who live in the places I've been. One of my favorite activities to do with my sister when we visit a new place is to roam up and down the aisles of a grocery store. We pick a favorite snack from each place we visit and compare it to the ones we've visited other places. My curious mind never stops. Who came up with this snack? When do they eat it? Why hasn't this snack become popular back home? This is the way my mind works.

The curious traveler is surprised by the ordinary. And the curious traveler learns that this kind of mindset helps them emotionally and practically. On an emotional level, a curious mindset gives you a more open, optimistic outlook when encountering the inevitable challenges that come with traveling away from home. Practically speaking, curiosity helps you solve problems. This might be as simple as figuring out the tipping practice where you are, or it might be figuring out what to do when you don't feel safe or are in the midst of a crisis.

It's often said that travel is the only expense that makes you richer. I couldn't agree more, as long as it's combined with curiosity and CQ.

 Travel – Curiosity = Blind

One of my friends says that tourists are like dogs in an art museum. They see everything and appreciate nothing. Traveling without curiosity means you miss what there is to see. And it often means overlooking the differences of a new place and overemphasizing the similarities to other places you've been.

Travel + Curiosity = Voyeur

On the other hand, traveling with unchecked curiosity runs the risk of being intrusive and naïve. This might mean going on slum tours and posting the pictures to social media or asking questions too soon or too aggressively. If you're simply chasing the adventure of satisfying your curious mind, your good intentions may be offensive or simplistic.

Curious Travel × CQ = Global Citizen

Research proves that travel plus curiosity combined with cultural intelligence is what ensures your travel investment keeps paying dividends. Cultural intelligence is a force multiplier. It's what translates your curiosity and overseas experiences into something with lasting value.

The study abroad student who travels with curiosity and CQ is able to talk to a potential employer about how their time in Rome, Cape Town, or Buenos Aires gives them a creative edge for doing the job.

The business traveler who travels with curiosity and CQ takes public transit back from a meeting in Shanghai and wanders the streets of a local neighborhood. They connect with colleagues and clients in a way that those sequestered in their hotels can't.

The traveler who brings curiosity and CQ engages in dialogue with the locals they visit in Dubai, Panama, and London. They have a different insight on the political riffs at home and abroad and can offer a more thoughtful perspective.

You can do this! Traveling isn't a trip, it's a life journey. There are amazing people everywhere. Let your next trip change you. When you travel, you convert more than money—you convert yourself. Don't give up. Plan your next trip now. Don't take the easy cruise. Build friendships through travel.

Curiosity, travel, and CQ have the power to promote understanding and collaboration among people who view the world in vastly different ways. I hope I've enticed you with the wonder of curious travel. It will enrich your discoveries in the moment and long after you're home. The connections and bonds formed as a curious traveler are the best benefit. I hope to meet you along the way.

 Bon Voyage!

Appendix

Ten Cultural Value Dimensions

One of the most helpful ways to process what you experience as a curious traveler is to understand some key cultural values that distinguish one group from another. Anthropologists and cross-cultural psychologists have developed a variety of cultural value dimensions to compare cultures. These value dimensions are most relevant when comparing different national cultures such as that of Germany versus Japan. But you'll also see these dimensions in a variety of other cultural contexts, including ethnic groups, regions across the same country, organizations, generations, and political parties.

Individuals have personal preferences along each of these cultural value dimensions. Sometimes your orientation reflects your culture of origin, but not always. A few of these are referenced throughout the book. If you aren't familiar with these concepts, they're a great starting point for building your cultural intelligence. The *Cultural Values Profile* offered through the Cultural Intelligence Center gives you feedback on your personal references for each of these dimensions compared to the dominant norms of the ten largest cultural groupings in the world.

Here's a brief description of ten of the most important cultural value dimensions.

Individualism versus Collectivism

Whether one favors Individualism or Collectivism is one of the most powerful differences in how we think, behave, and see the world. It is the extent to which you think of yourself primarily as an individual versus primarily as a member of a specific group (e.g., your family or work group).

INDIVIDUALISM	COLLECTIVISM
Emphasis on individual goals and rights	Emphasis on groups and personal relationships
Possible Indicators • Desire personal accountability • Say things like, "I'll take care of this."	**Possible Indicators** • First consideration is impact on in-group • Say things like, "Let me check with our team."
Working with Individualist People • Allow for autonomy • Recognize the importance of rapid decision-making	**Working with Collectivist People** • Create time for consultation and consensus-building • Recognize the importance of building lasting relationships

Individualist	Moderate	Collectivist
Anglo Germanic Europe Nordic Europe	Eastern Europe Latin Europe	Arab Confucian Asia Latin America Southern Asia* Sub-Saharan Africa
For a description of the ten cultural clusters listed above, see the information at the end of the appendix. *Indicates significant variation within cluster.		

Power Distance

Power Distance is the degree to which you prefer a flatter, egalitarian approach to leadership (Low Power Distance) as opposed to a more top-down, hierarchical approach (High Power Distance). The dominant norm in most cultures around the world is High Power Distance.

LOW POWER DISTANCE	HIGH POWER DISTANCE
Emphasis on equality and shared decision-making	Emphasis on differences in status; expect superiors to make decisions
Possible Indicators • Freely voice dissenting viewpoints to authority • Say things like, "Hey there" to someone more senior	**Possible Indicators** • Want to know the chain of command • Say things like, "Professor, Madam, or Doctor"
Working with Low Power Distance People • Deemphasize titles and formalities • Question or challenge authority	**Working with High Power Distance People** • Follow the chain of command carefully • Do not question authority, particularly in public

Low	Moderate	High
Anglo Germanic Europe Nordic Europe	Confucian Asia Eastern Europe* Latin Europe* Sub-Saharan Africa	Arab Latin America Southern Asia*
For a description of the ten cultural clusters listed above, see the information at the end of the appendix.		
*Indicates significant variation within cluster.		

Uncertainty Avoidance

Uncertainty Avoidance is the extent to which you prefer to reduce or avoid uncertainty versus being flexible and adapting to changing circumstances. Individuals with a Low Uncertainty Avoidance orientation prefer to figure things out as they go. Individuals with a High Uncertainty Avoidance orientation prefer to eliminate ambiguity and uncertainty through planning or tradition.

LOW UNCERTAINTY AVOIDANCE	HIGH UNCERTAINTY AVOIDANCE
Emphasis on flexibility and adaptability	Emphasis on planning and/or predictability
Possible Indicators • Comfortable with frequent change • Say things like, "I love a new challenge."	**Possible Indicators** • Rely on tradition or plans to eliminate uncertainty • Say things like, "Are we sure this will work?"
Working with Low Uncertainty Avoidance People • Avoid dogmatic statements • Invite them to explore solutions	**Working with High Uncertainty Avoidance People** • Give explicit instructions • Rely on formalized procedures and policies

Low	Moderate	High
Anglo Eastern Europe Nordic Europe	Arab Confucian Asia* Germanic Europe Southern Asia* Sub-Saharan Africa	Latin America Latin Europe
For a description of the ten cultural clusters listed above, see the information at the end of the appendix. *Indicates significant variation within cluster.		

Cooperative versus Competitive

This cultural value reveals your preferred way to achieve results, with a Cooperative orientation emphasizing a more collaborative, nurturing approach and a Competitive orientation emphasizing achievement and a more assertive approach to getting things done. A Cooperative orientation often emphasizes relationships first while a Competitive orientation often emphasizes tasks first.

COOPERATIVE	COMPETITIVE
Emphasis on collaboration and a nurturing approach	Emphasis on competition, assertiveness, and achievement
Possible Indicators • Want recognition for working well with others • Say things like, "I feel like our teams have really good chemistry."	**Possible Indicators** • Want recognition for achieving results • Say things like, "I am sure we can win this. We're the best!"
Working with Cooperative People • Establish relationship before task • Communicate to build rapport	**Working with Competitive People** • Focus on task first • Communicate to report information

Cooperative	Moderate	Competitive
Nordic Europe Sub-Saharan Africa	Arab Confucian Asia Eastern Europe Latin America Latin Europe Southern Asia*	Anglo Germanic Europe
For a description of the ten cultural clusters listed above, see the information at the end of the appendix. *Indicates significant variation within cluster.		

Time Orientation

This is not about punctuality. Time Orientation is the extent to which you prefer to focus on immediate results versus results that may come years later.

SHORT-TERM	LONG-TERM
Emphasis on immediate outcomes (success now)	Emphasis on planning (success later)
Possible Indicators • Emphasize what's coming up in the next few months • Say things like, "We need to demonstrate results quickly."	**Possible Indicators** • Emphasize the five- to ten-year implications • Say things like, "I'm interested in the long-term potential."
Working with Short-Term Time Oriented People • Prioritize "quick wins" • Focus on the present implications	**Working with Long-Term Time Oriented People** • Invest now for the future • Emphasize long-term implications

Short-Term	Moderate	Long-Term
Anglo	Germanic Europe	Confucian Asia
Arab	Latin America	
Eastern Europe	Latin Europe	
Nordic Europe	Southern Asia	
Sub-Saharan Africa		
For a description of the ten cultural clusters listed above, see the information at the end of the appendix.		

Context (Direct versus Indirect)

This cultural value focuses on direct versus indirect communication or Low versus High Context. This is the extent to which you prefer a direct, explicit approach to communicating compared to a more indirect approach that emphasizes harmony and saving face. A high context, indirect communicator pays attention to the context of the communication as well as the words. How is something said? What is not said? What is communicated by the way one dresses?

LOW CONTEXT (DIRECT)	HIGH CONTEXT (INDIRECT)
Emphasis on explicit communication (words)	Emphasis on indirect communication (tone, context)
Possible Indicators <ul><li>Depend on what is actually said or written</li><li>Say things like, "Can you be more specific?"</li></ul>	**Possible Indicators** <ul><li>Depend on tone, silence, and context to reveal meaning</li><li>Say things like, "Let me think about that."</li></ul>
Working with Low Context People <ul><li>Be direct and explicit</li><li>Focus on getting the message across clearly</li></ul>	**Working with High Context People** <ul><li>Recognize the importance of silence and reflection</li><li>Pay careful attention to what is not said</li></ul>

Low	Moderate	High
Anglo Germanic Europe Nordic Europe	Eastern Europe Latin America Latin Europe	Arab Confucian Asia Southern Asia* Sub-Saharan Africa
For a description of the ten cultural clusters listed above, see the information at the end of the appendix.		
*Indicates significant variation within cluster.		

153

Being versus Doing

Being versus Doing is the extent to which you emphasize enjoyment and quality of life versus achieving goals and being proactive. A Being oriented individual responds to things more reactively and passively whereas a more Doing oriented individual focuses on productivity and deliberately reaching goals.

BEING	DOING
Emphasis on quality of life	Emphasis on being busy and meeting goals
Possible Indicators <ul><li>Emphasize relationship over task</li><li>Say things like, "I love a holiday with nothing scheduled."</li></ul>	**Possible Indicators** <ul><li>Emphasize getting things done</li><li>Say things like, "We have so much planned for our holiday. I can't wait!"</li></ul>
Working with Being Oriented People <ul><li>Affirm the person and avoid focusing only on performance</li><li>Manage the relationship</li></ul>	**Working with Doing Oriented People** <ul><li>Affirm accomplishments and new opportunities</li><li>Manage the process</li></ul>

Being	Moderate	Doing
Arab	Confucian Asia*	Anglo
Latin America	Eastern Europe	Germanic Europe
Nordic Europe	Latin Europe	
Sub-Saharan Africa	Southern Asia*	

For a description of the ten cultural clusters listed above, see the information at the end of the appendix.

*Indicates significant variation within cluster.

Universalism versus Particularism

This is the extent to which you prefer to apply the same standards to everyone versus making exceptions for friends and family. Universalists emphasize established rules and standards that apply to all. Particularists emphasize unique standards based on specific circumstances and relationships.

UNIVERSALISM	PARTICULARISM
Emphasis on rules and standards that apply to everyone	Emphasis on unique standards based on specific relationships
Possible Indicators • Prefer standardized systems • Say things like, "That wouldn't be fair because we've never let anyone else do that."	**Possible Indicators** • Prefer taking things case by case • Say things like, "In light of the circumstances, we need to make an exception."
Working with Universalists • Provide commitments in writing and make every effort to abide by them • Provide rationale and advance warning for when circumstances require change	**Working with Particularists** • Demonstrate flexibility whenever possible • Invest in relationships and show the role of context in informing decisions

Universalist	Moderate	Particularist
Anglo Germanic Europe Nordic Europe	Eastern Europe Latin Europe	Arab Confucian Asia* Latin America Southern Asia Sub-Saharan Africa
For a description of the ten cultural clusters listed above, see the information at the end of the appendix. *Indicates significant variation within cluster.		

Expressiveness: Neutral versus Affective

Expressiveness is the extent to which you prefer to hide your emotions versus show them. Nonexpressive (Neutral) communicators emphasize nonemotional communication and tend not to share their feelings. Expressive (Affective) communicators emphasize expressive communication and tend to share their feelings openly.

NEUTRAL	AFFECTIVE
Emphasis on nonemotional communication and tendency not to share feelings	Emphasis on expressive communication and tendency to share feelings openly
Possible Indicators • Prefer a calm, cool reaction • Say things like, "There's no need to get all worked up about this."	**Possible Indicators** • Prefer an enthusiastic response • Say things like, "They looked uninterested in anything I had to say."
Working with Nonexpressive (Neutral) People • Manage emotions and regulate body language • Stick to the point in meetings and interactions	**Working with Expressive (Affective) People** • Open up to people and demonstrate warmth and trust • Work on being more expressive than might be typical

Neutral	Moderate	Affective
Confucian Asia Eastern Europe Germanic Europe Nordic Europe	Anglo* Southern Asia	Arab Latin America Latin Europe Sub-Saharan Africa
For a description of the ten cultural clusters listed above, see the information at the end of the appendix.		
*Indicates significant variation within cluster.		

Focus: Monochronic versus Polychronic

Focus is the extent to which you prefer to do one thing at a time versus multitasking. Individuals who prefer Monochronic (Linear) approaches focus on one thing at a time and keep their work and personal lives separate. Individuals who prefer Polychronic (Nonlinear) approaches shift their focus across different things at the same time and mix their work and personal life.

MONOCHRONIC	POLYCHRONIC
Emphasis on one thing at a time and keeping work and personal lives separate	Emphasis on multiple things at the same time and mixing work and personal lives
Possible Indicators • Prefer orderliness, structure, and punctuality • Say things like, "I need to work from home tomorrow so I can concentrate."	**Possible Indicators** • Prefer finishing a conversation over getting to the next appointment "on time" • Say things like, "Call me anytime. Even if it's the weekend."
Working with Monochronic (Linear) People • Provide follow-through and expediency when possible to build trust • When a deadline can't be met, propose an alternative one and stick to it	**Working with Polychronic (Nonlinear) People** • Find ways to be flexible on deadlines that are less important • Communicate relational impact if a deadline is not met

Monochronic	Moderate	Polychronic
Anglo Germanic Europe Nordic Europe	Confucian Asia* Eastern Europe Southern Asia	Arab Latin America Latin Europe* Sub-Saharan Africa
For a description of the ten cultural clusters listed above, see the information at the end of the appendix. *Indicates significant variation within cluster.		

Cultural Clusters

The cultural values orientations defined above can be grouped into cultural clusters where you're likely to find a significant presence of a specific cultural value. These clusters represent the ten largest cultural groupings in the world.

Cluster	Sample Countries
Anglo	Australia, Canada, New Zealand, United Kingdom, United States
Arab	Bahrain, Egypt, Jordan, Kuwait, Lebanon, Morocco, Saudi Arabia, United Arab Emirates
Confucian Asia	China, Hong Kong, Japan, Singapore, South Korea, Taiwan
Eastern Europe	Albania, Czech Republic, Hungary, Mongolia, Poland, Russia
Germanic Europe	Austria, Belgium, Germany, Netherlands
Latin America	Argentina, Bolivia, Brazil, Chile, Colombia, Costa Rica, Mexico
Latin Europe	France, French-speaking Canada, Italy, Portugal, Spain
Nordic Europe	Denmark, Finland, Iceland, Norway, Sweden
Southern Asia	India, Indonesia, Malaysia, Philippines, Thailand
Sub-Saharan Africa	Ghana, Kenya, Namibia, Nigeria, Zambia, Zimbabwe

Note: The countries are *not* the clusters themselves. They are simply places where you're likely to find a significant presence of the cultural clusters.

To learn more about these cultural value differences, check out my books, *Leading with Cultural Intelligence* and *Expand Your Borders*.

Acknowledgements

My life, my travels, and my writing are the culmination of so many generous contributions from people along the way. Most of these come from my dearest family and friends. But there is also no shortage of contributions from strangers I've encountered in my own curious travels near and far.

Let me explain it this way. We just returned from Ireland. My daughter Grace was involved in a serious cycling accident there and ended up having surgery. From the moment she was injured to our return back home, we experienced the beautiful generosity of people all along the way. Lilly and Eugene Ross, the Irish couple who were out for a hike on the path where we were biking, helped us get a rescue team to help Grace and then continued to stay by our side for hours, even coming back to the hospital multiple times to visit. Owen, the lead paramedic on site at the accident, not only administered drugs to alleviate Grace's pain but somehow managed to get her laughing. The list keeps going to include rescue teams, medical professionals, and staff from hotels and airlines who stepped up to help us, without us even knowing most of their names. And then of course our family and friends back home prepared for our arrival and helped us get Grace on the road to recovery.

This book is no different. It wouldn't be possible without my tribe. That list includes my incredible growing team at the Cultural Intelligence Center, not the least of whom is my assistant Kate Mondal who not only manages my chaotic life but read the book and offered her personal insights from her own travels. Linn Van Dyne, my partner at the Cultural Intelligence Center, dissects what I write and pushes me to make it better. My best friend and longtime confidante Steve Argue helped me from the conceptualization of the book all the way through to the final draft. In addition, I'm immensely grateful to a long list of colleagues and friends who read an early draft and offered feedback, including Steven Gillum, Amy Hunt, Adam King, Jessica Oldford, Giuliana Petrocelli, Cara Maas, Julie Slagter, Nic Weatherhead, and Edwin Yee. I incorporated so many of their rich suggestions on how to make the book better, deeper, and more accessible.

Beyond my tribe, there are countless people I've met along the way in traveling around the world who have a part in this book. Similar to the random, unexpected strangers who helped us in the midst of Grace's accident, I've met so many fascinating people across the globe whose voices, generosity, and friendship—even through a momentary encounter—have played a part in the ideas, experiences, and stories that fill these pages.

My greatest joy in all the world is traveling with my bride of more than 25 years and our two amazing daughters. Linda not only read a draft early on, she patiently talked through my ideas for the book over and over for months at a time. My daughter Emily offered me some of the most constructive input on the book I received from anyone. She's ventured off on many curious travels of her own now and teaches me as much as I teach her about what it means to be a culturally intelligent, curious traveler. Check out her travel blog at livermorelens.com. If there were pictures in a dictionary, I'm pretty sure my daughter Grace's photo would be next to the word *curious*. She's always chasing the next adventure, and she and I love to explore new foods and places together. And she used her artistic eye to create the cover art for the book.

I dedicated this book to my mom, who passed away while I was finishing it. I've traveled to more places internationally in the couple of months she's been gone than she ever did in her entire life. But she's the one who planted the seeds of curiosity in me. I miss her loving, inquisitive questions about where I've been and where I'm going next. But her curious spirit lives on.

Notes

Prologue

1 Mark Zuckerberg's commencement address at Harvard, May 25, 2017, *The Harvard Gazette*. https://news.harvard.edu/gazette/story/2017/05/mark-zuckerbergs-speech-as-written-for-harvards-class-of-2017/.

Chapter 1. The Power of Curiosity

1 Grant McCracken, *Chief Culture Officer: How to Create a Living, Breathing Corporation* (New York: Hachette, 2009), 119.

2 Julian Ryall, "DNA Proves Women Reunited via YouTube Are Twin Sisters," *The Telegraph*, February 12, 2014. http://www.telegraph.co.uk/news/worldnews/asia/southkorea/10632462/DNA-proves-women-reunited-via-YouTube-are-twin-sisters.html.

3 Matthew C. Canver et al., "Variant-Aware Saturating Mutagenesis Using Multiple Cas9 Nucleases Identifies Regulatory Elements at Trait-Associated Loci," *Nature Genetics* 49, no. 4 (2017): 625–634. doi:10.1038/ng.3793

4 M. J. Gruber, B. D. Gelman, and C. Ranganath, "States of Curiosity Modulate Hippocampus-Dependent Learning via the Dopaminergic Circuit," *Neuron* 84, no. 2 (2014): 486–496.

5 Todd Kashdan, *Curious: Discover the Missing Ingredient to a Fulfilling Life* (New York: HarperCollins, 2009), 3.

6 Sylvia Tomkins, *Affect, Imagery, Consciousness: Vol. 1, The Positive Affects* (New York: Springer, 1962), 17–19.

7 George Loewenstein, "The Psychology of Curiosity: A Review and Reinterpretation," *Psychological Bulletin* 116, no. 1 (1994): 75–98.

8 Angela Duckworth, *Grit: The Power of Passion and Perseverance* (New York: Scribner, 2016), 23.

9 Carol Dweck, *Mindset: The New Psychology of Success* (New York: Random House, 2006), 27–40.

10 Matthew A. Killingsworth and Daniel T. Gilbert, "A Wandering Mind Is an Unhappy Mind," *Science* 330 (2010): 932.

11 Kashdan, *Curious*, 40.

12 Daniel Gilbert, *Stumbling on Happiness* (New York: Random House, 2006).

13 Susan Smalley and Diana Winston, *Fully Present: The Science, Art, and Practice of Mindfulness* (Philadelphia: Lifelong Books, 2010), 42.

14 Kashdan, *Curious*, 173.

15 Kashdan, *Curious*, 199.

Chapter 2. The Power of Cultural Intelligence

1 Cultural Intelligence Research (Grand Rapids, MI: Cultural Intelligence Center), https://culturalq.com/about-cultural-intelligence/research/.

2 Katie Bain, "The Rise of Donald Glover: How He Captured America," *The Guardian*, May 12, 2018. https://www.theguardian.com/music/2018/may/12/the-rise-of-donald-glover-childish-gambino.

3 Yuval Noah Hurari, *21 Lessons for the 21st Century* (New York: Random House, 2018), 319.

4 Napoleon Chagnon, *Noble Savages: My Life Among Two Dangerous Tribes—the Yanomamö and the Anthropologists* (New York: Simon & Schuster, 2013), 153.

5 Emily Eakin, "How Napoleon Chagnon Became Our Most Controversial Anthropologist," *New York Times*, February 13, 2013. http://www.nytimes.com/2013/02/17/magazine/napoleon-chagnon-americas-most-controversial-anthropologist.html?_r=0.

6 Chagnon, *Noble Savages*, 118.

7 Graeme Wood, "Anthropology, Inc.," *The Atlantic*, March 2013. http://www.theatlantic.com/magazine/archive/2013/03/anthropology-inc/309218/.

8 Ibid.

9 Sherry Turkle, *Reclaiming Conversation: The Power of Talk in a Digital Age* (New York: Penguin Books, 2016), 37.

10 Turkle, *Reclaiming Conversation*, 45.

11 Sara H. Konrath, Edward O'Brien, and Courtney Hsing, "Changes in Dispositional Empathy in American College Students over Time: A Meta-analysis," *Personality and Social Psychology Review* 15, no. 2 (2011): 180–198.

12 Jacob Stol, "Taylor Swift Puts 'Emotional' Letter to Fans in Hard Copies of New Album Reputation," *The Independent*, November 12, 2017. https://www.independent.co.uk/arts-entertainment/music/news/taylor-swift-new-album-reputation-emotional-letter-fans-kanye-west-feud-tom-hiddleston-a8050706.html.

Chapter 3. Dilemma: Where's the Queue?

1 Laura Pedersen, "Everyone Line up: Canada's Tradition of Orderly Queuing 'Foreign and Strange' to Many Newcomers," *National Post*, July 25, 2014.

2 Gregory David Roberts, *Shantaram* (New York: St. Martin's, 2004), 105.

3 Denise Winterman, "Queueing: Is It Really the British Way?," *BBC News Magazine*, July 4, 2013. http://www.bbc.com/news/magazine-23087024.

4 Oscar Lewis, "The Culture of Poverty," *Scientific American* 215, no. 4 (October 1966): 21.

5 Brian Christian and Tom Griffiths, *Algorithms to Live By: The Computer Science of Human Decisions* (New York: Henry Holt, 2016), 83.

6 Minda Zetlin, "Rude Drivers Who Merge at the Last Second Are Doing You a Favor, according to Science," *Inc.*, July 1, 2017. http://inc-asean.com/the-inc-life/rude-drivers-merge-last-second-favor-according-science/.

7 Paul Hiebert, *Anthropological Reflections on Missiological Issues* (Grand Rapids, MI: Baker, 1994), 114.

Chapter 4. Dilemma: Do I Eat the Eye?

1 Jennifer 8. Lee, "The Hunt for General Tso," TED Talk, July 2008. https://www.ted.com/talks/jennifer_8_lee_looks_for_general_tso?language=en.

2 R. I. Stein and C. J. Nemeroff, "Moral Overtones of Food: Judgments of Others Based on What They Eat," *Personality and Social Psychology Bulletin* 21 (1995): 480–490.

3 P. Rozin and D. Schiller, "The Nature and Acquisition of a Preference for Chili Pepper by Humans," *Motivation and Emotion* 4 (1980): 77. https://doi.org/10.1007/BF00995932

4 J. D. Vance, *Hillbilly Elegy: A Memoir of a Family and Culture in Crisis* (New York: HarperCollins, 2016), 210.

5 Vance, *Hillbilly Elegy*, 212.

Chapter 5. Dilemma: You Have 84 Kids?

1 "The Perils of Polygamy: How Plural Marriage Begets Violence," *Economist*, December 23, 2017, 24–26.

2 Gabriele Leow, "Have You Eaten?" https://www.youtube.com/watch?v=Wfm2gXULEIw&feature=youtu.be.

3 Maya Thiagarajan, *Beyond the Tiger Mom: East-West Parenting for the Global Age* (Hong Kong: Tuttle, 2016).

4 Adam Davidson, "The Boomerang Kids Won't Leave," *New York Times Magazine*, June 20, 2014, 15–17.

5 Zac Dychtwald, *Young China: How the Restless Generation Will Change Their Country and the World* (New York: Macmillan, 2016), 72.

6 Chagnon, *Noble Savages*, 324.

7 Chagnon, *Noble Savages*, 217.

8 "The Perils of Polygamy: How Plural Marriage Begets Violence," *Economist*, December 23, 2017, 24–26.

9 Maura Kelly, "What's So Crazy about an Arranged Marriage?," *Atlantic*, May 1, 2012. https://www.theatlantic.com/entertainment/archive/2012/05/whats-so-crazy-about-an-arranged-marriage/256561/.

Chapter 6. Dilemma: Why Does "Yes" Mean "No"?

1 Neil Miller, "One Tip to Become Indispensable in Cultural Communication," *Learning India*, March 26, 2014. http://learningindia.in/case-for-indirect-communication/.

2 John Hooker, "Cultural Differences in Business Communication." http://public.tepper.cmu.edu/jnh/businessCommunication.pdf.

3 Erin Meyer, *The Culture Map: Breaking through the Invisible Boundaries of Global Business* (New York: Public Affairs, 2014), 62–64.

4 Juliane House, "Communicative Styles in English and German," *European Journal of English Studies* 10, no. 3 (2006): 249–267.

5 Thomas Talhelm et al., "Large-Scale Psychological Differences Within China Explained by Rice Versus Wheat Agriculture," *Science* 344, no. 6184 (2014): 603–608. doi:10.1126/science.1246850

6 Richard Nisbett, *The Geography of Thought : How Asians and Westerners Think Differently and Why* (New York: Free Press, 2003).

Chapter 7. Dilemma: What Do You Mean by "Now"?

1 Katherine Fan, "Japanese Train Commits Truly Inexcusable Error," *The Points Guy*, May 15, 2018. https://thepointsguy.com/news/japanese-train-commits-truly-inexcusable-error-of-departing-25-seconds-early/.

2 Harriet Mallinson, "Be Half an Hour Late in Greece but Bang on Time in Japan: How Different Nations across the Globe Value Punctuality Revealed," *Daily Mail*, July 26, 2016. http://www.dailymail.co.uk/travel/travel_news/article-3708645/Be-half-hour-late-Greece-bang-time-Japan-different-nations-globe-value-punctuality-revealed.html.

3 Elizabeth Davies, "Unlocking the Secret Sounds of Language: Life without Time or Numbers," *The Independent*, May 7, 2006.

4 Philip Zimbardo, *The Time Paradox: The New Psychology of Time That Will Change Your Life* (New York: Free Press, 2008).

5 Brent Lindeque, "South African Time Explained: Just Now vs. Now Now," *Good Things Guy*, January 24, 2018. https://www.goodthingsguy.com/fun/south-african-time-explained/.

6 R. W. Brislin and E. S. Kim, "Cultural Diversity in People's Understanding and Use of Time," *Applied Psychology: An International Review* 52 (2003): 363–382. doi:10.1111/1464- 0597.00140

7 Kaushik Basu and Jörgen W. Weibull, "Punctuality, a Cultural Trait as Equilibrium," The Research Institute of Industrial Economics, June 10, 2002.

8 Mihaly Csikszentmihalyi, *Flow: The Psychology of Optimal Experience* (New York: HarperCollins, 1990), 9.

9 E. A. Holman and Philip Zimbardo, "The Social Language of Time: The Time Perspective–Social Network Connection," B*asic and Applied Social Psychology* 31 (2009): 136–147.

Chapter 8. Practices of the Curious Traveler

1 Winifred Gallagher, *Rapt: Attention and the Focused Life* (New York: Penguin, 2009), 1–2.

2 Kashdan, *Curious*, 3.

3 Kashdan, *Curious*, 80.

4 Smalley and Winston, *Fully Present*, 149.

5 Kashdan, *Curious*, 52.

6 Craig Storti, *The Art of Crossing Cultures* (Yarmouth, ME: Intercultural Press, 1990), 95.

7 George Loewenstein, "The Psychology of Curiosity."

8 Ibid.

9 Sandi Mann and Rebekah Cadman, "Does Being Bored Make Us More Creative?" *Creativity Research Journal* 26, no. 2 (2014): 165–173.

10 Amelia Hill, "Boredom Is Good for You," *The Guardian*, May 6, 2011. https://www.theguardian.com/science/2011/may/06/boredom-good-for-you-claims-study.

11 Malcolm Gladwell, *Blink: The Power of Thinking Without Thinking* (New York: Back Bay Books, 2005), 166.

12 P. Christopher Earley, Soon Ang, and Joo-Seng Tan, *CQ: Developing Cultural Intelligence at Work* (Stanford, CA: Stanford University Press, 2006), 11.

13 Charles S. Carver and Michael Scheier, *On the Self-Regulation of Behavior* (Cambridge, UK: Cambridge University Press, 1998). Also see A. J. Elliot and H. A. McGregor, "Test Anxiety and the Hierarchical Model of Approach and Avoidance Achievement motivation," *Journal of Personality and Social Psychology* 76 (1999): 628–644.

14 Guihyun Park, Linn Van Dyne, and Daniel Ilgen, "Satisfaction Pursuing Approach and Avoidance Goals: Effects of Regulatory Fit and Individual Temperaments," *Motivation and Emotion* 37, no. 3 (2013): 424–432.

15 Ibid.

16 Csikszentmihalyi, *Flow*, 3.

17 Duckworth, *Grit*.

18 Kashdan, *Curious*, 60.

19 Christopher K. Hsee and Ruan Bowen, "The Pandora Effect: The Power and Peril of Curiosity," *Psychological Science* 27, no. 5 (May 2016): 659–666.

Chapter 9. Tips for the Curious Traveler

1 Megan Leonhardt, "Anthony Bourdain's Guide to Great Travel," *Money*, April 2018, 45.

2 Leonhardt, "Bourdain's Guide," 45.

Made in the USA
Columbia, SC
05 May 2022

59993691R00102